Predictive Coding Guru's Guide

Technology • Statistics • Workflows

Core Concepts
Innovative Workflow
Practical Guidance

Rajiv Maheshwari

Predictive Coding Guru's Guide
by Rajiv Maheshwari

www.predictivecodingguide.com

Credits:
> Cover design by Anete Bukovska
> Typesetting based on Legrand template from latextemplates.com

First printing, May 2013

ISBN-13:978-0-989-38500-8

Contents

Preface

If you are reading this book, then it is fair to assume that you are interested in the subject of predictive coding. What makes predictive coding so exciting is that various branches of mathematics and science – algebra, vector algebra, matrix theory, set theory, probability theory, trigonometry, information theory, and statistics – come together to solve a business problem. Perhaps you have some idea what predictive coding is about, or perhaps you are an expert in predictive coding and just wondering what this book is about. Chances are most people would be somewhere in between. I have tried to write this book with the spirit of "keeping it as simple as possible, but no simpler" – a quote attributed to Albert Einstein. One of the main goals of this book is to be accessible and useful to a broader audience that includes anyone who is involved in eDiscovery or interested in application of supervised machine learning. Beginners will find a good overview of the business context and the key drivers for the use of predictive coding, a systematic introduction of core concepts in statistics and machine learning technology, a detailed description of currently used workflows, and finally an innovate workflow that brings all the pieces together to present a solution for the future. People who have had some experience with predictive coding would find a wealth of information that debunks the black box syndrome including an in-depth conceptual understanding of how predictive coding works and the scientific proof that supports the validity of predictive coding results. The experts will find the greedy workflow and the testing performed on a real pre-coded dataset, without the knowledge of responsiveness criteria, particularly interesting. My guess is that the greedy workflow will be immediately subjected to critical testing and analysis. I hope that this book promotes widespread adoption of this fantastic technology.

Although I would recommended reading the chapters in sequence, the text is also intended as a reference book. The book is organized as follows:

Chapter 1 eDiscovery and Predictive Coding provides a high level overview of the litigation process and eDiscovery, introduces predictive coding, and compares it to other information retrieval technologies commonly used in the industry.

Chapter 2 Technology Behind Predictive Coding introduces basic mathematical concepts that are essential to understanding how machine learning works, describes a general framework of steps followed by most machine learning algorithms used for predictive coding, and explains three of the popular algorithms in greater detail.

Chapter 3 Applying Statistics to Predictive Coding covers core concepts essential to applying and interpreting statistics to predictive coding correctly, provides the proof that statistics can be scientifically applied to predictive coding of documents, and offers guidance on how to avoid common errors and pitfalls.

Chapter 4 Predictive Coding Workflows provides a lucid explanation of the two general workflow approaches – *Assisted Review Workflow* and *Suggested Review Workflow* – currently used in the industry in several derivative forms, describes the key challenges with both the approaches, and introduces an innovative workflow – *the greedy workflow.*

Appendix A Test Results on Real Dataset provides detailed test results of applying the greedy workflow on a real pre-coded dataset that excluded Excels.

Appendix B Test Results on Excel Dataset provides summary of test results of applying the greedy workflow on a real pre-coded dataset containing only Excels.

Conventions

Important terms and definitions are highlighted in **bold** or *italic*. The terms classification, categorization, tagging and coding are used synonymously in the book and imply identifying a document as belonging to a particular category such as responsive, non-responsive, etc.

Companion Website

Readers are encouraged to visit www.predictivecodingguide.com for additional information/errata, questions, comments and reviews.

Acknowledgements

First of all, I would like to thank my parents who worked very hard to offer me the best possible opportunities. I would like to thank my brother Vaibhav Maheshwari for always raising the bar. The idea that I should do some applied research and write a book was partly inspired by his PhD thesis. I would like to thank the rest of my immediate family for their incessant support and encouragement. Most importantly, I would like to thank my lovely girlfriend Anete Bukovska for her patience and support through the excruciating six months I had to work late nights and weekends to complete the research, testing and writing of this book.

Special thanks to my friends and colleagues Sujan Bajracharya and Maclean Almeida. This book would have taken a lot longer to finish without Sujan's help with testing and Maclean's help with creating the companion website. And finally, thanks to several of my friends, especially Bimal Tamrakar, for always motivating me to work on some cool stuff.

About the Author

Rajiv Maheshwari has recently joined Micros as VP of product development. Prior to joining Micros, Rajiv was director of global engineering at Integreon, a leading provider of integrated legal solutions, where he headed the development of software products & applications. In addition to his work in legal industry, Rajiv has designed innovative technology solutions for retail / eCommerce and financial services over the last 15 years. His interests in technology include information retrieval, eCommerce and cloud computing. He enjoys golf, snowboarding and traveling around the World.

1 eDiscovery and Predictive Coding

This chapter provides a high level overview of the litigation process and eDiscovery for the readers who may be new to the industry. The review stage is the most important stage of eDiscovery and makes up for the majority of the total cost. Hence, review has always been the focus of innovation with new applications of cutting edge information retrieval technologies. Predictive coding has gained significant momentum in the last few years because of its ability to automatically tag majority of the documents that would otherwise need to be manually reviewed. The chapter defines predictive coding and compares it to other information retrieval technologies commonly used in the industry. Limitations of both the searching approach as well as the predictive coding approach are discussed. Finally, statistics is introduced as a valuable tool for eDiscovery.

Overview of Litigation Process

Generally speaking, there are two types of legal cases or lawsuits. **Criminal lawsuits** involve a charge prosecuted by a government body that some individual or entity broke a criminal law and should be punished. **Civil lawsuits** involve disputes between individuals or other entities including government entities, where damages or a remedy is requested. These different types of cases involve different burden of proof and different procedures. Civil lawsuits generally proceed through the following four stages: pleadings, discovery, resolution, and possibly an appeal.

Pleadings

In a lawsuit the parties could be plaintiffs, defendants, applicants, petitioners or respondents, but they are all considered **litigants** during an ongoing trial. In most, but not all cases, the litigants may represent themselves in a lawsuit. The litigants may also retain legal counsel, in which case their attorneys are referred to as **litigators**.

In civil cases, the **plaintiff** is the party who brings the lawsuit and the **defendant** is the party who is being sued. A civil action is started by the plaintiff filing a **complaint** with the court. The complaint is served on the defendant along with **summons**. The defendant is given a specific amount of time to file an answer to the complaint. The **answer** provides the defendant's side of the dispute. The defendant may also file **counter-claims** against the plaintiff, alleging that the plaintiff has harmed the defendant and should be held liable for that harm. There may be a few iterations with amended complaints and amended answers. The complaint and the defendant's answer together form **pleadings**. The pleadings inform each party of the claims of the other and specify the disputed issues. Depending upon the complexity of the lawsuit, other pleadings and parties may be added. The pleadings serve as a framework for later proceedings.

Discovery

After the pleadings stage is completed, the legal process enters into the discovery stage, where either the plaintiff or the defendant may initiate the request for information from the other parties or witnesses in the lawsuit. While discovery allows the parties to obtain more facts about the incident, the rules and the judge prevent one party from harassing another party or a witness with requests for unnecessary information. The discovery rules also make sure that **privileged information** (communications that ordinarily may not be disclosed in court) is safeguarded, and that only relevant matters are discoverable.

The discoverable information may include interrogatories (written questions that must be answered in writing), depositions (oral questions, given under oath) that are usually recorded in an official transcript, paper documents, physical evidence, and electronic evidence. With the prolific use of modern communication and information management systems, more and more data is in electronic format (often referred to as **electronically stored information** or **ESI**) such as emails, electronic documents, electronic calendars, databases, voicemails, videos, etc. There are two special requirements for electronic evidence:

1. Exact image copy of the evidence is obtained
2. It can be proven that nothing has been altered or changed from the time the image copy was obtained. This is typically demonstrated via **chain of custody**, i.e. chronological documentation (or paper trail), showing the seizure, custody, control, transfer, analysis, and disposition of the evidence.

The discovery process balances the need for accuracy in finding the facts with the need for fair treatment of all parties to the lawsuit. Typically, the judge presiding over the case sets deadlines and guidelines for certain stages of discovery to keep the case progressing efficiently.

The litigation may involve complex factual issues concerning areas such as medicine, finance, engineering, etc. A claim or defense may require support from an **expert** to explain technical information or validate an argument during the discovery stage. The expert may work in the capacity of an **expert consultant**, and assist the parties and the court with no obligation to give **expert testimony**. The expert may also be **expert witness** who is called to testify and give **expert opinions** on certain complex factual issues.

Resolution

After the discovery stage, the case moves towards resolution. A case may be resolved in various ways, including dismissal, settlement, or judgment following a trial. After finding out more facts in discovery, the plaintiff may dismiss the lawsuit entirely or a certain defendant from the lawsuit. The court may dismiss the case if a party has not followed the timing instructions, or if there is a legal basis to dismiss the case. The parties may decide to settle the case by agreeing to the amount of damages or a remedy. If the parties have not dismissed or settled the case, then it may be resolved following a trial before a judge, or a judge and a jury.

Appeal

Following a trial, a party dissatisfied with the result may appeal. During an appeal, a party asks a higher court to review the trial court proceeding. The parties present their arguments in briefs, which are submitted to the appellate court along with the record of evidence from the trial court. The appellate court usually reviews a case for legal error only. Except under unusual circumstances, the appellate court will not review factual evidence or override a jury's findings of fact. The appellate court announces its decision in a document called an opinion. The appellate court will affirm the verdict if it finds that there was no error in the trial court proceeding. However, if there was an error, the appellate court can reverse the verdict or order the trial court to conduct a new trial.

Overview of eDiscovery

eDiscovery is the popular term for discovery of electronically stored information (ESI) to be used as evidence in a civil lawsuit. A number of different people may be involved in an eDiscovery project: lawyers and legal professionals from the litigant parties, forensic specialists, data processing and review specialists, information technology professionals, record managers and project managers, among others. eDiscovery heavily uses information technologies such as data extraction technologies that support hundreds of types of file formats, database systems; data storage systems; information retrieval technologies; workflow and review applications; data conversion and imaging; computer networks and internet.

Electronic Discovery Reference Model (EDRM)

The Electronic Discovery Reference Model (EDRM) shown in *Figure 1.1* provides a conceptual framework consisting of various stages in the eDiscovery process. The model provides standards and guidelines for the development, selection, evaluation and use of electronic discovery products and services. The completed model was placed in the public domain in May 2006. Detailed information on EDRM can be obtained online at www.edrm.net. The various stages in EDRM are briefly described below:

1. **Information Management** addresses managing the entire IT infrastructure that supports the eDiscovery process starting with the creation of ESI to its use, retention, archival and final disposition. This stage covers policies and processes that enable IT efficiency, information

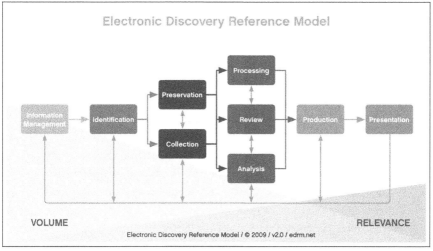

Figure 1.1: *Electronic Discovery Reference Model v2.0*

security, risk management, legal risk management as well as business profitability.

2. **Identification** is locating potential sources of ESI & determining its scope, breadth, and depth. This stage involves identifying the data sources via data mapping, key witnesses and custodians, key timeframes, keyword lists, potentially relevant documents and data types, and internal/external data storage systems such as document repositories, file servers, email systems, disaster recovery systems, etc.

3. **Preservation** is ensuring that ESI is protected against inappropriate alteration or destruction. It is usually done by isolating and protecting potentially relevant data in a legally defensible way that also mitigates risks.

4. **Collection** is the acquisition of potentially relevant ESI as defined in the identification stage in a legally defensible manner. Forensic analysis and methodology is used to ensure defensibility.

5. **Processing** is reducing the volume of ESI and converting it, if necessary, to forms more suitable for review, analysis and other tasks. Full text data and metadata (such as email header information, file dates, author names, etc.) is extracted from native files and container files such as zip files, files containing embedded files, Outlook PST, etc. Various tools are used to identify file types, character encoding, language detection, entity extraction, etc. Data is further culled (re-

moving clearly non-relevant files) based on criteria such as file type, date range, etc. Culled data is processed to identify duplicate files, near-duplicates, and conversation threads. Full text and metadata is indexed in search engines that support advanced keyword search and conceptual search. Some of these steps could be performed in the review platform in the next stage.

6. **Review** is evaluating ESI to identify relevant documents to produce and privileged documents to withhold. In the review stage, the processed documents are typically "hosted" in a review platform that provides advanced tools and capabilities via its application user interface to make the review process easier. Features supported by the review application include various types of document folders, tagging, annotations, universal viewer for native files, extracted metadata and text viewer, redactions, advanced search, clustering, predictive coding, multiple user roles, customizable workflows for manual review, printing documents to Tiff, import/export, privilege log creation and advanced reporting.

7. **Analysis** is evaluating ESI for content & context, including key patterns, topics, people & discussion. Although analysis is identified as a separate stage in EDRM, it could be potentially performed across all stages to increase productivity. In the initial stages of EDRM, analysis can be used to develop information management approach, fact finding and scoping of potentially relevant ESI. During the collection and processing stage, analysis can be used to estimate time, effort and cost; early case assessment; and selection of tools and technology. During the review stage, analysis can be used to enhance review process and improve review quality and speed. At all stages, analysis can be used for validation/quality assurance, risk management, and reporting key metrics.

8. **Production** is delivering ESI to opposing parties in appropriate forms, using appropriate delivery mechanisms, and in compliance with agreed production specifications and timelines. Rule 26(f) of the Federal Rules of Civil Procedure requires that the parties must agree on the method and format by which ESI is to be produced early on in the discovery process. The documents are produced in their native format; near-native format in which the files are converted into a searchable format that approximates the native format; image formats such as tiff and pdf; or paper format. Bates numbering, stamps and redactions are applied to image files or paper if required. Searchable text is produced in plain text files. The extracted metadata is produced

in delimited text files, in a markup language format such as EDRM XML load file, or in a proprietary load file format. The load file links all the produced deliverables together and allows easy upload to litigation support application's database.

9. **Presentation** is displaying ESI before audiences (at depositions, hearings, trials, etc.), especially in native & near-native format, to elicit further information, validate existing facts or positions, or persuade an audience.

Review Stage of eDiscovery

The review stage is the most important stage of eDiscovery and makes up for the majority of the total cost. Simply speaking, the review stage consists of identifying responsive documents (i.e., relevant documents) to produce and privileged documents (attorney-client communication or work product) to withhold. The eDiscovery project may require relevant documents be further tagged with various issue codes. The overall goal of the review process is to do it cost-effectively and minimize mistakes. Traditionally, the documents are reviewed and tagged by humans. The human review process is performed in two stages – first level review and second level review. First level review, often performed by paralegals and contract attorneys, pertains to identifying responsive documents. Second level review, often conducted by senior level reviewers/attorneys, includes issue tagging, identifying privileged documents, and a second pass to crosscheck the responsive documents identified in the first level review.

A research conducted by the RAND Institute for Civil Justice (ICJ), a research institute within RAND Law, Business, and Regulation (LBR) and published in 2012, employed a case-study method to gather cost data for 57 large-volume e-discovery productions, including those in traditional lawsuits and regulatory investigations. One of the key findings was that traditional human review makes up the largest percentage, typically about 73%, of all eDiscovery production costs. The study also found that review costs are difficult to reduce significantly if the review is conducted in the traditional manner due to the following reasons:

- Significant reduction in current labor costs is unlikely.
- Increasing the speed of review has its limits.
- Techniques for grouping documents would probably not foster sufficiently dramatic improvements in review speed for most large-scale

reviews.

- Human reviewers are highly inconsistent.

The high cost of traditional review is not the only challenge. The volume of ESI continues to grow and eDiscovery projects involving millions of documents are becoming increasingly common. In such cases, traditional human review becomes not only cost prohibitive but also impractical. Various technologies such as advanced keyword-search, conceptual-search, near-duplicates identification, email thread, and clustering along with workflow batching have been used to make the review process faster, efficient and more accurate. Predictive coding is the latest addition to the growing list of information retrieval technologies being used in eDiscovery and has become a hot topic of interest in the last couple of years.

Commonly Used Information Retrieval Technologies

This section briefly describes information retrieval technologies that have been commonly used in eDiscovery over the last several years.

Full-text Indexing and Searching

All text and metadata is extracted from the documents and indexed in a computer data structure such as inverted file index, suffix trees, or signature files. Then we can perform simple search queries consisting of words, phrases or text, as well as complex search queries such as a structured Boolean query with several nested Boolean expressions and the "and", "or" and "not" operators. The search results are typically displayed sorted by relevance to the search query with a link to the relevant document, summary text and additional useful metadata. Modern search engines used in eDiscovery also support several advanced features, such as:

- Fuzzy search, which returns approximate matches to the queried field's value.
- Proximity search, which allows searching by proximity of two words (or "terms" in general) within a specified distance.
- Query expansion, which enables retrieving more matching documents by expanding the user query with additional terms such as word synonyms, other morphological forms of the words, and fixing spelling errors.
- Sorting by any number of fields, and by complex functions of numeric fields

- Highlighted context snippets
- Faceted searching based on unique field values, explicit queries, date ranges, numeric ranges or pivot
- Multi-select faceting by tagging and selectively excluding filters
- Spelling suggestions for user queries
- "More like this" suggestions for a given document
- Auto-suggest functionality for completing user queries

Keyword searches typically yield low precision (proportion of truly responsive documents to all the documents in the search results) and low recall (proportion of truly responsive documents in the search results to all the responsive documents in the dataset), because many words could have the same meaning (referred to as **polysemy**) and the same word could have different meanings (referred to as **synonymy**). However, full-text searching continues to be the most widely used information retrieval tool in eDiscovery. The queries, the search results, and the relationship between the two can be easily explained. It still happens to be the best tool when searching for exact text, highly specific Boolean query, alphanumeric or numeric values, specific field values, range searches, etc.

Clustering

Clustering is a type of unsupervised machine-learning technique, where the algorithm tries to discover clusters of similar documents in the dataset. Unlike supervised machine-learning, there are no pre-defined categories and example documents. The objective of clustering is descriptive rather than predictive. Most significant words in each cluster are used for topic labeling of the respective cluster. The two popular methods of clustering are hierarchical and partitioning.

The **hierarchical** method recursively groups documents into a hierarchy of clusters based on a measure of document similarity. The depth of the hierarchy can be specified by the user or constrained by a similarity (relevance) threshold value. One of the disadvantages of hierarchical clustering method is that a document committed to a particular cluster node cannot be moved to another cluster. Hence, adding significant number of new documents to the dataset typically requires clustering the entire dataset again.

The **partitioning** method starts from an initial partition of the dataset into the desired number of clusters k, which needs to be specified by the user, and then iteratively moves the documents between the k clusters until certain optimization criteria is achieved. While the partitioning method does not have the same disadvantage as the hierarchical method and it is comparatively faster, it is very sensitive to noisy data and outliers, and the optimality of the cluster depends upon the selection of initial partition.

However, clustering continues to be an important tool in eDiscovery. It is often used to get a high level understanding of the dataset and key topics, especially if the topical words are meaningful. It can be potentially used to batch clustered documents in a review workflow. It can also be used for stratified sampling, which may improve estimation of properties in some datasets.

Concept Searching

Concept searching matches documents to the query based on the similarity of *concepts* in them rather than keywords or terms, thereby addressing the issue of synonymy and polysemy in keyword searches.

Similar Documents Searching

This technique searches for documents that are similar to a given document. The given document is treated as a query against the search index, which could be a keyword search index or a concept search index. The number of documents returned in the search result can be controlled by a similarity (relevance) threshold value specified by the user.

Near Duplicates

Many software products in the market consider finding near duplicates as a specialized case of similar documents searching where the relevance threshold is set to a very high value by the user. There are other algorithms also that are specifically designed to identify near duplicates via other approaches.

Conversation Threading

This technique assembles a conversation thread from individual emails identifying replies, forwards, copying, spawning of new conversations, as well as any missing emails in the thread. Some email systems such as Outlook Exchange and Lotus Notes use a conversation index field to keep track of conversation threads. However, it may not be reliable if there are emails in the dataset from other email systems. Hence, algorithms that perform text analysis to assemble conversation threads are used sometimes.

Depending upon the discovery criteria and case protocol, it is sometimes possible to isolate and bulk-code a group of documents using one or more of the above technologies. However, the observed accuracy is generally poor with significant number of documents misclassified as responsive or non-responsive. Hence, these technologies have been mostly used to identify, folder and batch documents for manual review via various workflows. The traditional workflow strategies are generally aimed at expediting the review process by batching similar documents to the same reviewer, or suppressing documents those are duplicates, near duplicates, or contained in another document.

What is Predictive Coding?

Predictive coding is the process of using a smaller set of manually reviewed and coded documents as examples to build a computer generated mathematical model that is then used to predict the coding on a larger set of documents. It is a specialized application of a class of techniques referred to as supervised machine-learning in computer science. Other technical terms often used to describe predictive coding include document (or text) "classification" and document (or text) "categorization". This book also uses the terms "coding" and "tagging" synonymously.

Predictive coding process requires the following elements: example documents, feature training documents, test documents, a preprocessor, a supervised machine-learning algorithm, and algorithm specific parameters.

Example Documents

Example documents are documents that are reviewed and categorized manually into a finite set of categories. It is assumed that the categories are mutually exclusive and the examples are uniquely categorized, i.e., no example document is categorized into more than one category. It is also assumed that the example documents have content that can be processed by the preprocessor. Example documents are conventionally referred to as training documents in computer science. However, this book uses the term "example documents" to avoid confusion with feature training documents.

Feature Training Documents

Feature training documents are a representative subset (or could be the entire dataset) of the corpus of documents that are being categorized using predictive coding. They are used by the preprocessor to extract important features that describe the documents in the dataset. For example, the features can be words, phrases or a group of words.

Test Documents

Test documents are all the documents that need to be predictively coded. They are conventionally referred to as "test documents" because the machine-learning algorithm is "trained" on the training documents and "tested" on the test documents.

Preprocessor

Preprocessor is a computer program that processes example documents, feature training documents, and test documents, and converts them into a format suitable for the machine-learning algorithm. It is usually embedded into the predictive coding software and hence, transparent to the end user.

Supervised Machine-Learning Algorithm

Supervised machine-learning algorithm is one or a combination of machine-learning algorithms used to build the mathematical (predictive) model based on the distribution of features observed in the training documents. The algorithm then analyses the features in each test document and uses the predictive model to predict the test document's category.

Algorithm Specific Parameters

Most algorithms allow user to specify a relevance threshold parameter that specifies the minimum relative value of similarity measure (e.g., 85%) that the test documents are required to have to their predicted category's training documents set. If a test document does not meet relevance threshold for any of the defined categories, it is left uncategorized. Different algorithms offer other parameters that enable users to tweak their behavior and/or performance.

Searching vs. Predictive Coding

Searching is a top-down approach as illustrated in *Figure 1.2*. We start with understanding the guidelines for responsive and non-responsive documents (and other issue codes). Then we build queries that fetch documents for those specific categories. We could take some help from technology such as the advanced search features discussed before in this chapter, but query building is mostly a manual process. The queries can be thought of as "classifiers" of documents into the defined categories. We verify the search results to check the accuracy. We iterate the process as many times as necessary and sufficient.

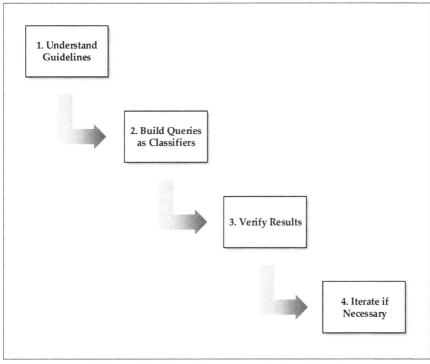

Figure 1.2: *Searching approach (top-down)*

On the other hand, predictive coding is a bottom-up approach as illustrated in *Figure 1.3*. We start with understanding the guidelines for responsive and non-responsive documents (and other issue codes). We observe some of the documents via sampling or some other method to discover example documents for each of the categories. Then, we use a supervised machine-learning algorithm, which detects patterns in the examples and builds a predictive model that contains one or more classifiers. The classifiers are used to perform categorization on the remaining documents in the dataset. Finally, we verify the categorization results to check the accuracy. We iterate the process as many times as necessary and sufficient.

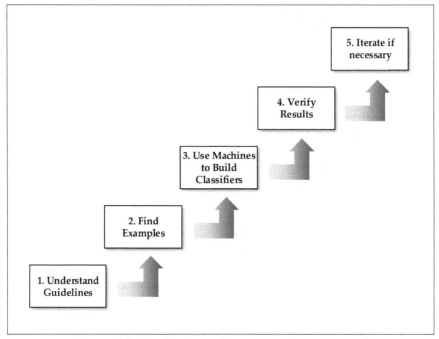

Figure 1.3: Predictive coding approach (bottom-up)

The key difference is how the classifiers that identify and separate the documents into various categories are build – manually by humans using the searching approach, or automatically by the machine using the predictive coding approach.

Limits of Searching Approach

Building a query for a given category such that it fetches a natural language document if and only if it belongs to the category is a difficult task for the following key reasons:

- Natural languages are inherently ambiguous and ambiguity is what makes them a powerful means of communication. Ambiguity can be intentional or unintentional. While human brain is able to resolve the ambiguities almost subconsciously using the context and drawing on our general knowledge and experience, it is often non-trivial to convert the reasoning into a search query.
- Query languages are limited in terms of the expressions and semantics they can support. While some techniques such as word sense dis-

ambiguation and query expansion can be utilized to improve search results, the overall accuracy remains relatively low with the tradeoff being between precision and recall.

Limits of Predictive Coding Approach

Predictive coding approach is based on inductive learning, i.e., learning by example and then generalizing it. It is important to note that inductive reasoning is probabilistic. It only states that, given the premises, the conclusion is probable. For example, if all observed animals with golden fur and stripes were tigers, inductive reasoning would imply that any animal with the same characteristic is likely a tiger. The generalization precludes the possibility that the animal could be a cat, and there could be a white tiger. The key take away is that the machine-learning algorithms can only generalize based on the features they have learnt and the examples they have observed. Hence, the accuracy of predictive coding in large part depends on feature selection and the quality of examples.

The Winner

Searching approach tends to perform better when discovery criteria is such that accurate queries can be developed with a few iterations. Machine-learning approach tends to perform better when language ambiguity is expected or we are dealing with very large number of documents that could make a top-down searching approach combined with a linear review infeasible.

A real-life eDiscovery project would likely benefit from using a combination of both top-down as well as bottom-up approaches. The greedy workflow, introduced in this book, tilts the balance in favor of predictive coding, especially for large and complex datasets.

Why Statistics?

Any time we identify a group of documents using any of the information retrieval technologies and bulk-code them without manually reviewing each of them, we want to have a certain degree of confidence that those documents indeed belong to the coded category. Statistics enables us to confirm the coding accuracy at the desired confidence level by reviewing only a sample of randomly selected documents from the group. Statistics can also be used to examine a very large dataset for interesting properties, such as the estimated proportion of responsive documents in the dataset, by reviewing a much smaller random sample of documents. Thus, statistics is a powerful tool for eDiscovery. It is very important to understand how statistical principles work in order to apply them correctly and interpret the results correctly.

2 Technology Behind Predictive Coding

This chapter explains the machine-learning technology that powers predictive coding. It is important to have a functional understanding of the technology in order to make the best use of it. The chapter introduces basic mathematical concepts that are essential to understanding how machine-learning works. There are several data analysis techniques and machine-learning algorithms that can be used for predictive coding. Although these algorithms use different mathematical approaches, they typically follow certain common steps. These common steps are described in a general framework to help in conceptual understanding of the technology. Three of the most popular algorithms used for predictive coding – k-Nearest Neighbor, Support Vector Machines, and Latent Semantic Analysis – are described in detail along with their advantages and disadvantages. Some of the other commonly used algorithms are described briefly. Finally, the chapter addresses the question of how to choose the best algorithm.

Basic Concepts

Scalars and Vectors

A scalar is a quantity that only has magnitude, for example, mass or temperature. On the other had, a vector is a mathematical object that has magnitude and direction. Vectors are represented by a line of a given length pointing along a given direction, and denoted by a bold faced character or a character with an arrow on top (i.e., $\mathbf{A}$ or $\vec{A}$). The magnitude of a vector is its length and is normally denoted by $|A|$ or simply A. A vector can be moved freely in space and remains the same as long as its magnitude and direction are the same. *Figure 2.1* illustrates same vector at three different positions.

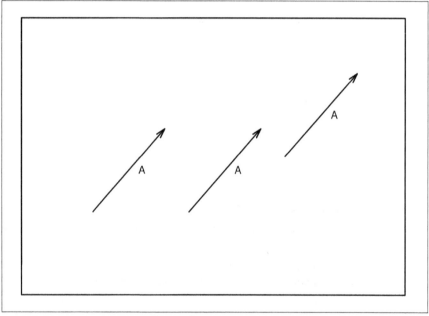

Figure 2.1: *Same vector*

Figure 2.2 illustrates three different vectors. Addition of two vectors is accomplished by placing the vectors head to tail in sequence to create a triangle such as shown in *Figure 2.3*.

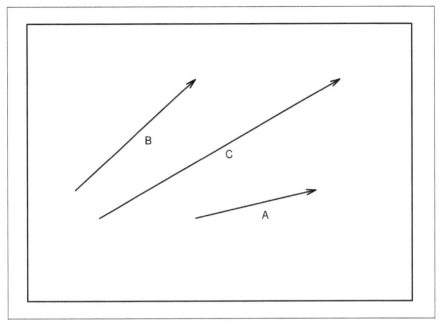

Figure 2.2: *Different vectors*

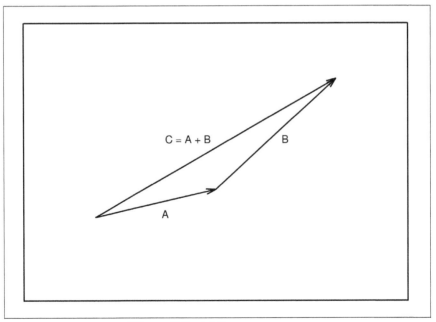

Figure 2.3: *Adding two vectors*

Unit Vectors and Vector Components

Most people are familiar with a point plotted on a two dimensional graph with x-axis and y-axis, and the origin of the graph where $x = 0$ and $y = 0$. If an arrow is drawn from the origin to the point on the graph, the arrow represents a vector because it not only captures the distance of the point from the origin but also the direction with respect to the reference axes.

A vector $\vec{C}$ on the graph can be decomposed into two component vectors $\vec{A}$ and $\vec{B}$ along the x-axis and the y-axis, respectively, such that

$$\vec{C} = \vec{A} + \vec{B}$$

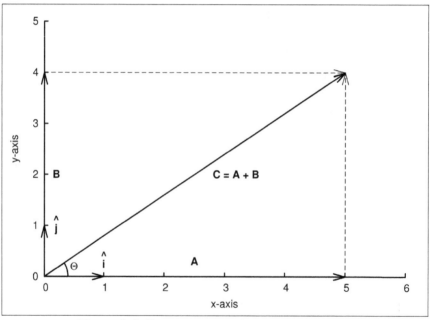

Figure 2.4: Base vectors and vector components

Vectors $\vec{A}$ and $\vec{B}$ are referred to as **base vectors** for the reference axes. A **unit vector** is a vector of length equal to one and denoted by a lower case letter with a ' ^ ' on top. $\hat{i}$, $\hat{j}$, and $\hat{k}$ are typically used to represent the unit vectors for the x-axis, y-axis, and z-axis respectively. A vector is equal to the product of its length and the unit vector along its direction. Hence, vectors $\vec{A}$, $\vec{B}$, and $\vec{C}$ in *Figure 2.4* can be specified in terms of unit vectors $\hat{i}$ and $\hat{j}$ as follows:

$$\vec{A} = A_x\hat{i} \quad \text{where } A_x \text{ is the length of vector } \vec{A}$$
$$\vec{B} = B_y\hat{j} \quad \text{where } B_y \text{ is the length of vector } \vec{B}$$
$$\vec{C} = A_x\hat{i} + B_y\hat{j}$$

Note that the above representation of vector $\vec{C}$ is similar in the form to linear algebraic representation "ax + by". Specifying vectors in terms of component unit vectors allows us to apply linear algebra making it easier to perform computations. The same vector $\vec{C}$ can also be specified in terms of a different set of 3-dimensions (3 reference axes) – x, y and z – as illustrated in *Figure 2.5* below:

$$\vec{C} = C_x\hat{i} + C_y\hat{j} + C_z\hat{k}$$

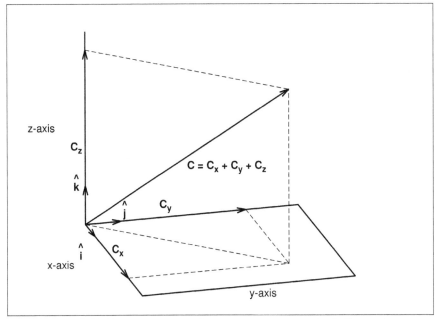

Figure 2.5: *Base vectors and vector components in 3-dimensions*

The 3 dimensions x, y and z are commonly used as reference axes that are perpendicular (orthogonal) to each other because several objects can be easily described in terms of length, breadth and height. Orthogonality can be generalized to n dimensions representing non-overlapping, uncorrelated, or independent attributes of any kind. Given any number n of reference axes (i.e., n-dimensions), it is possible to describe a given vector in space in terms of the sum of component base vectors of each of the n dimensions. For example, we could describe vector $\vec{A}$ in a 5-dimensional vector space as follows:

$$\vec{A} = A_v \hat{g} + A_w \hat{h} + A_x \hat{i} + A_y \hat{j} + A_z \hat{k}$$

If $A_v = A_w = 0$, then $\vec{A}$ lies in x-y-z 3-dimensional plane. Similarly, if $A_v = A_w = A_x = 0$, then $\vec{A}$ lies in y-z 2-dimensional plane. If $A_v = A_w = A_y = A_z = 0$, then $\vec{A}$ lies on the x-axis and is 1-dimensional. In general, dimensions represent attributes that we are interested in. If we are analyzing only shapes of objects, we may consider 3 dimensions – length, width and height. On the other hand, if we are interested in the shapes and colors of objects, we may add a fourth dimension – color – to our vector space.

Vector Space Model

Let's consider each of the following 3 quotes in *Table 2.1* as documents:

Doc ID	Document Content
001	As far as the laws of mathematics refer to reality, they are not certain, and as far as they are certain, they do not refer to reality. – Albert Einstein
002	The essence of mathematics is not to make simple things complicated, but to make complicated things simple. – S. Gudder
003	If people do not believe that mathematics is simple, it is only because they do not realize how complicated life is. – Tobias Dantzig

Table 2.1: Example documents

Let's assume that the above documents were processed through a filter program. The filter program provided base forms of the words of interest to us as output and filtered out everything else including the names. The result of the filtering process can be described as shown in *Table 2.2*:

Doc ID	Document Content (Filtered)
001	law, mathematics, reality, certain, certain, reality
002	essence, mathematics, simple, thing, complicated, complicated, thing, simple
003	people, mathematics, simple, complicated, life

Table 2.2: Extracted terms from example documents

If we consider each unique word as a dimension and its frequency (the number of times it occurs) as length, we can represent the occurrence of word in a given document as a base vector, and the document as a vector equal to the sum of base vectors corresponding to each unique word in the document. *Table 2.3* below shows the above documents represented in terms of our chosen 10 dimensions corresponding to the 10 unique filtered words in our example dataset of 3 documents:

Doc ID	law	mathematics	reality	certain	essence	simple	thing	complicated	people	life
001	1	1	2	2	0	0	0	0	0	0
002	0	1	0	0	1	2	2	2	0	0
003	0	1	0	0	0	1	0	1	1	1

Table 2.3: Example document-term matrix

The above matrix is referred to as **Document-Term matrix** (or **Term-Document matrix** in its transposed form.) We use **term** instead of **word** because a term can be used to represent a word, a phrase, an n-gram, or some other linguistic entity. Terms are assumed to be stochastically independent. The technique of representing text documents as vectors in a multi-dimensional space is referred to as **Vector Space Model (VSM)**. The 10 dimensions in the above simplistic example constitute the vector space model and each of the documents is a vector in the vector space.

Vector space model serves as the foundation of information retrieval theory. It is used in information filtering (e.g., collaborative filtering approach used by recommendation systems employed at many online shopping websites), information retrieval (e.g., Web search engines), and relevance rankings (e.g., clustering and classification.) Sophisticated predictive coding algorithms build an advanced vector space model via the steps illustrated in *Figure 2.6* and described below.

1. **Text extraction**. Full text is extracted from the documents via a separate processing system. Most predictive coding algorithms assume document text is available in appropriate format.
2. **Term extraction**. The text processing for term extraction may include the following:
   - **Tokenization**: document text is broken up into words, phrases, symbols, or other meaningful elements called tokens.
   - Removing HTML, XML, other mark-up tags
   - Removing **stopwords**: frequently used words that carry little useful information, for example, pronouns, prepositions and conjunctions.
   - Performing **word normalization**: the process of grouping words that are likely to be equivalent in the context of the information retrieval problem domain. For example, the words swim, swimmer and swimming have conceptual related meaning, and hence, can be represented (or normalized) by the word swim. Word normalization can significantly reduce the number of redundant terms. There are three types of word normalization techniques:
     - **Morphological stemming**: terms such as 'retrieving' are reduced to the root word stem 'retriev'.
     - **Lexicon-based**: terms such as 'retrieval' become 'retrieve'.
     - **Term clustering**: classes are used such that terms 'recover', 'fetch' and 'bring' are all equivalent values.
3. **Term weighting**: a numerical function that defines unit of measure for the terms (dimensions) is used. Basic weighting schemes include **term frequency (tf)** – the number of times a term occurs in a docu-

ment, **inverse document frequency (idf)** – inverse of the proportion of documents that contain a given term, **tf*idf** (tf multiplied with idf).

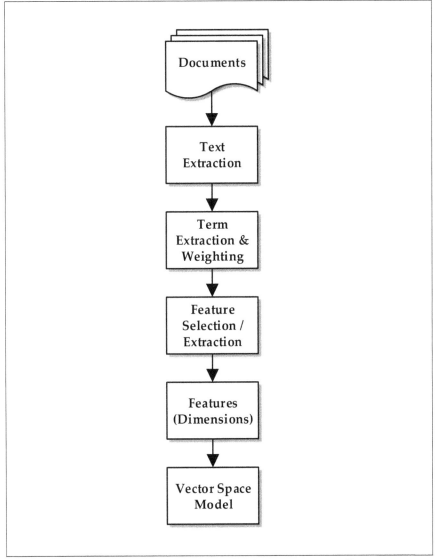

Figure 2.6: *Vector Space Model (VSM) process flow*

4. **Dimensionality reduction**. A central problem in text classification is the high dimensionality of the vector space. A dataset in an eDiscovery project could contain thousands of unique words even after stopwords removal and word normalization. Using every unique

word as a dimension will make predictive coding computationally complex and cost prohibitive in terms of both processing time and resources. Not all unique words based terms are useful as dimensions. Moreover, the set of terms could also be mathematically transformed into a different set of terms, such as "concepts", that are more suitable predictors of document category. The finally selected or transformed terms are used as dimensions of the vector space model and referred to as **features**. Features can be thought of as abstract characteristics that describe the documents in the vector space model and help classify documents into the defined categories. The process of reducing the initial set of terms to most important features is referred to as dimensionality reduction. Dimensionality reduction techniques can be divided into two main groups:

- **Feature selection**. In feature selection, the non-informative terms are removed from the documents by choosing a subset of K dimensions that provide the most useful information out of the M original dimensions. The remaining (M minus K) dimensions are discarded.

- **Feature Extraction**. In feature extraction, also referred to as re-parameterization, the process finds a new set of K dimensions that are combinations of the original M dimensions. Use of this technique in Latent Semantic Analysis (LSA) is discussed later in this chapter.

Document Similarity

Now that we have discussed a simple way of representing documents as vectors in a multi-dimensional space, we can use geometric and trigonometric functions, and linear algebra to calculate various measures of document similarity.

A simple similarity measure is the **Euclidean distance** defined as the ordinary distance between two points. The Euclidean distance between two documents is defined as the distance between the end points of the corresponding document vectors in the multi-dimensional vector space. Two documents are more similar to each other if the Euclidean distance between them is smaller.

Another commonly used document similarity measure is the **cosine similarity**. In trigonometry, the value of cosine of angle between two sides of a triangle varies between 0 and 1. The smaller the angle, the closer the value of cosine is to 1, the bigger the angle, the closer the value of cosine is to 0. The cosine of angle between two document vectors is called as cosine similarity and given by the following formula:

$$sim(A,B) = \frac{\vec{A} \cdot \vec{B}}{|A||B|}$$

General Approach to Document Categorization

While there are several supervised machine-learning algorithms and each of them may use somewhat different mathematical approach, they all utilize the following three common steps:

1. **Feature training**. This step creates the vector space model suitable for the learning algorithm and the classification task as shown in *Figure 2.7*. In order to create the dimensions of the vector space model, the algorithm needs to identify most useful features to model the entire dataset. Typically, a large subset of the entire dataset (for example, 10% random sample or 10,000 documents whichever is greater) is sufficient to extract the features. The sample subset is referred to as the **feature training set** in this book. The entire dataset could also be used as feature training set, however, it may take longer to process. The feature training set is processed through the steps described in the previous section. The result is the final set of component features constituting the vector space model.

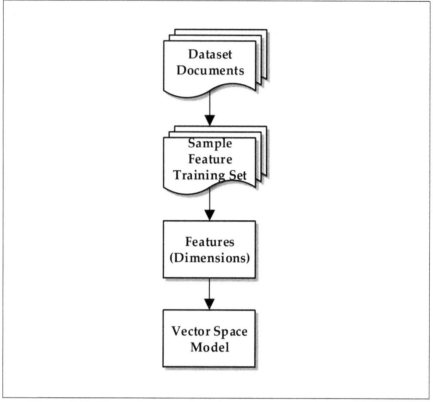

Figure 2.7: *General approach to document categorization - Feature training*

2. **Example training**: This step is illustrated in *Figure 2.8*. The classification categories are defined and example documents are provided for each of the categories. These set of documents are collectively referred to as **example set** in this book. The predictive coding algorithm learns from examples, hence it is important to make sure that examples belong to one and only one of the defined categories. The documents in the example set go through the same processing described in the previous section and converted into vectors made up of component features of the vector space model developed in step 1. The result is a feature-document matrix for all the example documents. Then the predictive coding algorithm develops one or more classifier functions for the defined categories. Classifier functions for some of the popular predictive coding algorithms are explained in later sections of this chapter. The vector space model and the classi-

fiers together constitute the **predictive model**. The predictive model specifications can be typically saved to a file, which is sometimes referred to as **categorization index** by some vendors.

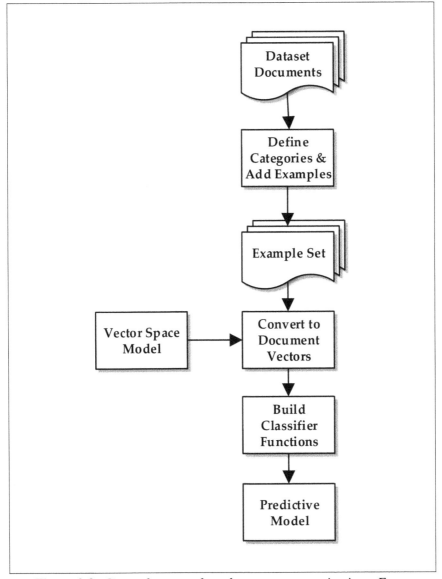

Figure 2.8: *General approach to document categorization - Example training*

3. **Testing**: This step is illustrated in *Figure 2.9*. The predictive model, which is already trained on examples in the previous step, is used to categorize a new set of documents into the defined categories. This step is conventionally referred to as **testing** because the predictive model is "tested" for prediction accuracy on documents that it has not seen before, and the documents being categorized are referred to as **test documents**.

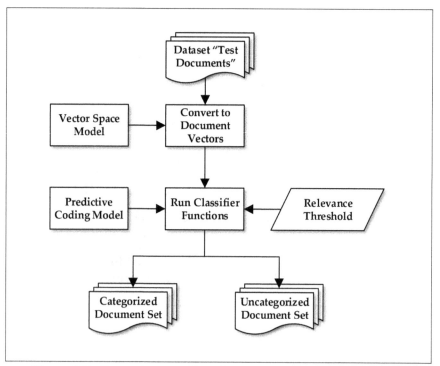

Figure 2.9: *General approach to document categorization - Testing*

Before the predictive model can be applied, the test documents go through the same processing described in the previous section and converted into vectors made up of component features of the vector space model developed in step 1. The result is a feature-document matrix for all the test documents. Then the predictive coding algorithm runs the classifier functions developed in the previous step to compute every test document's similarity score (**relevance score**) to the defined categories. If the documents can be categorized in only one category, the document is predicted to belong to the category with the highest similarity score. If the documents can be categorized in multiple categories, then the predictive coding software provides a relative measure such as classification probability for various categories. The software allows specifying a minimum **relevance threshold** value. The documents that do not meet the relevance threshold for any of the defined categories are labeled as "uncategorized".

k-Nearest Neighbor (kNN)

k-Nearest Neighbor (kNN) is one of the simplest algorithms which categorizes a document based on the assigned categories of the closest k example documents in the vector space. The metric that defines how close a document is to its neighbor can be based on any similarity measure such as Euclidean distance or Cosine similarity. Each of the k nearest neighbors gets to cast a vote for its category. The category with the majority vote is the predicted category. *Figure 2.10* below shows vector space model with examples and test documents.

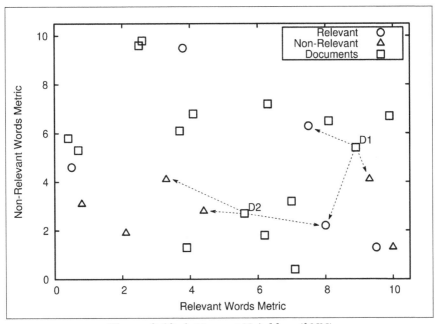

Figure 2.10: k-Nearest Neighbor (kNN)

The ○ points represent the examples for Relevant documents, the △ points represent examples for Non-Relevant documents, and the □ points represent test documents. For $k = 3$, the test document D1 has two Relevant example documents and one Non-Relevant example document as its three closest neighbors. Hence, D1's predicted category is Relevant. On the other hand, the test document D2 has one Relevant example document and two Non-Relevant example documents as its three closest neighbors. Hence, D2's predicted category is Non-Relevant.

In the above example, each of the k nearest neighbor documents is given equal weight regardless of its distance (similarity) to the test document. The similarity score of each neighbor document to the test document could be used to weight its category vote in order to use weighted-sum voting instead of majority voting. Test documents are sorted by their predicted category relevance score, and the documents that do not meet the minimum relevance threshold value are left uncategorized. Using higher value of k decreases the chance that the decision will be unduly influenced by a noisy training example close to the document being predicted. However, large values of k also reduce the acuity of the method. If kNN is used in a predictive coding workflow (see *Chapter 4*), the value of k can be tuned until the categorization effectiveness is optimized on the control set.

Advantages & Disadvantages

The advantage of kNN is that it is simple to understand. Despite its simplicity, it has been found to be among the top performing methods in text categorization evaluation. kNN is scalable to large datasets and the cost of re-training (i.e., when categories or training documents are changed) is relatively low compared to some of the other algorithms.

One disadvantage of majority voting based classification is that the classes with more examples tend to dominate the prediction. Unless the algorithm employs techniques to address this problem, it is possible that kNN categorization can result in poor accuracy in an iterative predictive coding workflow.

Another disadvantage of kNN is that its accuracy can be severely degraded by the presence of noisy or irrelevant features, or if the feature scales are not consistent with their importance. Hence, kNN based algorithms should use advanced techniques that improve feature selection and scaling.

Support Vector Machines (SVM)

A support vector machine is a statistical based learning algorithm that analyzes data and recognizes pattern. Its objective is to find a decision surface that best separates the data points belonging to two different classes in the vector space.

Let's consider a set of documents where we have identified all the keywords that are Relevant as well as all the keywords that are Non-Relevant as part of our feature selection process. For the sake of simplicity, let's assume we performed re-parameterization by combine all the relevant words into a single attribute – Relevant Words Metric – whose value is defined by the proportion of the number of occurrences of relevant words over the total number of words in a given document, and the attribute is scaled to the range $0 - 10$. So, for example, if a document has 15 occurrences of relevant words in a total of 60 words, then the Relevant Words Metric is equal to $15/60 \times 10 = 2.5$. Similarly, let's assume we defined another re-parameterized feature Non-Relevant Words Metric for the non-relevant words in the document. Then, we selected a subset of the documents as examples, reviewed and tagged them as Relevant or Non-Relevant, and processed them so that each example document can be represented via a 2-dimensional data point consisting of (Relevant Words Metric, Non-Relevant Words Metric).

Figure 2.11 shows a 2-D scatter plot of the example documents. The relevant examples are represented via ○ points, whereas the non-relevant examples are represented via △ points. A support vector machine can be trained to identify the best possible decision surface that separates the relevant examples from the non-relevant examples. The decision surface would be a line or more generally a curve in the case of a 2-dimensional vector space. *Figure 2.11* shows one such line that separates relevant from non-relevant examples. Now, we can use this separating line for predicting the category of a new document, which has not been reviewed, by representing the document in the same 2-dimensional vector space. If the new document's data point representation falls above the line it is Non-Relevant, if it falls below the line it is Relevant, and if it falls too close to the line it can be labeled uncategorized. It is possible to identify several separating lines as shown in *Figure 2.12*, and then the question is how to find the optimal separating line.

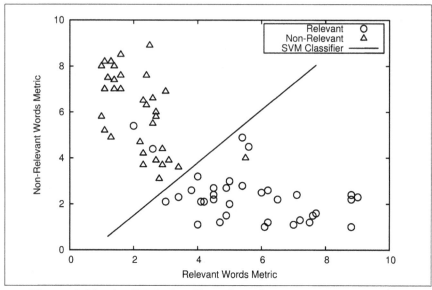

Figure 2.11: *An SVM classifiers for relevant/non-relevant documents in 2-dimensional VSM*

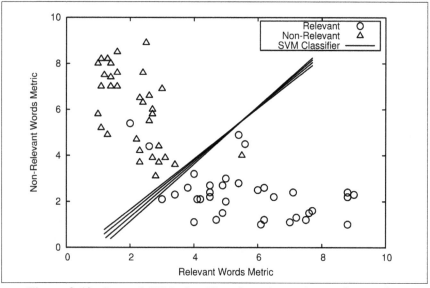

Figure 2.12: *Several SVM classifiers for relevant/non-relevant documents in 2-dimensional VSM*

SVM finds the optimal separating line by selecting the one that provides maximum distance from the nearest point on both sides (i.e., both categories) identified by support vectors. This approach is referred to as the maximum margin approach.

The optimal separating line was able to separate most of the points belonging to the two categories but there were few points that fell into the other category. These are referred to as outliers. It is not uncommon to find outliers. In fact, real datasets can be seldom cleanly separated into classes. SVM allows a user specified soft margin that controls roughly how many examples and how far they are allowed to be on the other side of the separating line. *Figure 2.13* below shows outliers and SVM maximum margin.

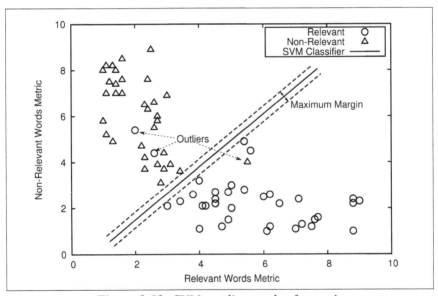

Figure 2.13: SVM: outliers and soft margin

Let's assume we decided to add a third attribute based on bag of all other words, i.e., words in the document set other than those identified as Relevant and Non-Relevant. Then, we processed the example documents again so that each example can be represented via a 3-dimensional data point consisting of (Relevant Words Metric, Non-Relevant Words Metric, Other Words Metric). *Figure 2.14* below shows a 3-D scatter plot of the documents. The Non-Relevant documents are represented via the cluster of △ points on top, whereas the Relevant Documents are represented via the cluster of ○ points at the bottom. Instead of a separating line, we have a separating hyperplane.

Thus, the generalized approach of SVM is to find an optimal hyperplane that separates the data points in an n-dimensional vector space into two labeled categories. In real life scenario, documents are usually represented in terms of several features in an n-dimensional vector space where n is a large number.

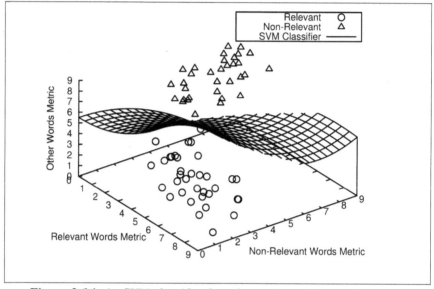

Figure 2.14: *An SVM classifier for relevant/non-relevant documents in 3-dimensional VSM*

Another interesting thing to note in the above figure is that the data points that were not cleanly separable earlier in a two dimensional space (because of the few outliers) can now be cleanly separated in a 3-dimensional space via a hyperplane. This shows that it is possible to find a better separating hyperplane by adding dimensions to the vector space model for a given dataset. Dimensions can be added via additional attributes such as the case in the above example, or using special mathematical functions known as Kernel Functions.

Adding Dimensions

Additional dimensions can be useful, however, it is important to assess their value as good predictors. The dimension "Other Words Metric" in our example is not a good predictor since presumably it has no correlation with either Non-Relevant or Relevant documents. While it may result in a high training accuracy on example set, it can potentially misclassify test Relevant documents that have too many "other" words as Non-Relevant and test Non-Relevant documents that have fewer "other" words as Relevant. This shows that feature selection is a very important step in building a good predictive model.

Kernel Functions

Kernel functions are mathematical functions that provide an easy way to project data points from a lower dimensional vector space (where we are unable to find a good separating hyperplane) to a higher dimensional vector space (where we could potentially find a good separating hyperplane). It is possible to prove that for a given set of uniquely categorized data points (i.e., none of the data points have more than one category label), there exists a kernel function that will allow the data points to be cleanly separated. However, there could be two potential issues.

Curse of dimensionality

As the number of dimensions increases, the number of possible separating hyperplanes also increases, but exponentially. Hence, it becomes computationally more difficult for any algorithm to find the optimal solution.

Over fitting

The projected hyperplane from higher dimensional vector space could be so specific to the examples that it would result in misclassification of test documents even if they were slightly different from the example documents. This effect is referred to as over fitting and is not unique to SVM. It can also happen with other machine-learning algorithms.

Advantages & Disadvantages

The advantage of SVM is that learning is more robust and over fitting is not common. SVM works well even with fewer training examples. It is more tolerant to errors in examples and the prediction accuracy is generally high.

The disadvantage of SVM is that it is impossible to tell which example document or documents influenced the category prediction of a specific test document. This information can be useful in predictive coding workflow (see *Chapter 4*).

Latent Semantic Analysis (LSA)

Latent Semantic Analysis (LSA) is based on the assumption that there is some underlying or latent structure in the pattern of word usage across documents and that statistical techniques can be used to estimate this structure referred to as **concepts**. It also assumes that words that are close in meaning will occur in similar pieces of text. LSA when used in the context of information retrieval is referred to as **Latent Semantic Indexing (LSI)**. There is no difference between LSA and LSI in terms of the fundamental approach.

LSA tries to address two problems in the vector space model representation of documents:

- **Synonymy**: same thing can be referred to by many different words or phrases, e.g. car and automobile. This leads to poor recall.
- **Polysemy**: most words have more than one distinct meaning, e.g. model, chip. This leads to poor precision.

(There are other techniques to address the above two problems, and they can be used with other predictive coding algorithms such as kNN and SVM.)

A high level description of LSA algorithm and its application to document classification is as follows:

1. Data is preprocessed to build a word-document matrix (more generally term-context matrix) of dimensions $m \times n$, i.e., m words by n documents. This is similar to the example in *Table 2.3*.
2. Matrix entries are converted to weights. The weight for each entry is typically the product of a local term weight, which describes the relative frequency of the word in the document, and a global weight, which describes the relative frequency of the word within the entire collection of documents.
3. Singular Value Decomposition (SVD) technique is applied to divide the word-document $m \times n$ matrix into 3 matrixes:
   (a) Word-concept matrix $m \times r$
   (b) Singular matrix $r \times r$
   (c) Concept-document (transposed) matrix $r \times n$
       Essentially, this step transforms the word "in a" document relationship into word "in a" concept and concept "in a" document relationships.

4. The LSI modification to standard SVD in step 3 is to further reduce the r concepts into k most significant concepts (and hence, k dimensions), thereby preserving the most important semantic information in the text while reducing noise and other undesirable artifacts of the original vector space. So, we get two useful matrices m words $\times$ k concepts and k concepts $\times$ n documents that essentially form the semantic space. This semantic space can be used for concept based searching, clustering, and classification.

5. Document similarity is computed based on concepts by applying any similarity measure, such as Euclidian distance or Cosine similarity, to the k concepts $\times$ n documents matrix. After the concept-document matrix is created, a classification algorithm such as kNN can be used to classify documents based on concepts.

Advantages & Disadvantages

LSA has been shown to outperform co-occurrence models and simple vector space models. Since LSI does not depend on literal keyword matching, it is especially useful when the text data is noisy, as in OCR (Optical Character Recognition) text or spelling errors.

LSA is computationally intensive and requires significant amount of memory – typically the entire categorization index needs to be loaded into main memory. Hence, LSA does not scale well for very large datasets. Another issue in LSA is finding optimal dimensionality k for the semantic space. Prediction accuracy improves as dimensionality is increased until it hits optimal point, then slowly decreases until it hits standard vector model. Finding the optimal point can be computationally intensive.

Other Algorithms

There are several other classification algorithms and extensions to the algorithms discussed in this Chapter. Some of the other popular algorithms are briefly described in this section.

Rocchio's algorithm is the classic method for document routing or filtering in information retrieval. In this method, a prototype vector is built for each category and a document is classified by calculating its similarity to the vector representing each category. The prototype vector for a given category is computed as the average vector over all training document vectors that belong to that category. The learning process is very fast for this algorithm.

Naïve Bayes algorithm uses the joint probabilities of words and categories to estimate the probabilities of categories given a document. The naïve part is the assumption of word independence, i.e. the conditional probability of a word given a category is assumed to be independent from the conditional probabilities of other words given that category. This assumption makes the computation far more efficient than the exponential complexity of other classifiers because it does not use word combinations as predictors.

Decision trees based classification consists of a collection of decision rules (e.g., if A then "yes", otherwise "no"), which are created during a procedure known as recursive partitioning. For example, if variable x is Relevant Words Metric and variable y is Non-Relevant Words Metric as used in example to illustrate SVM, then a highly simplified rule can be: if $x > 3$ then Relevant; else if $y > 3$ then Non Relevant, else Relevant.

The decision tree for the example is illustrated in *Figure 2.15*.

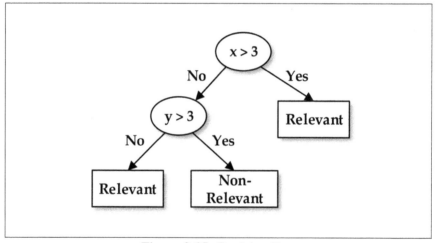

Figure 2.15: Decision Tree

In principle, the number of possible decision trees grows exponentially with the number of attributes. Hence, finding the optimal tree can be computationally intensive. However, efficient decision tree based algorithms use a greedy strategy to develop the tree based on making a series of locally optimum decisions, and achieving a reasonably accurate decision tree in a reasonable amount of time. One of the advantages of decision trees is that they are simple to understand and interpret.

In addition to several algorithms for machine-learning and classification, there are several techniques for feature extraction and selection, training data sampling, and classifier training. A combination of various techniques and algorithms is often employed in order to improve classification accuracy for a given dataset.

Choosing The Best Algorithm

It would be fantastic if it were possible to identify the single best algorithm that could be used in all situations. However, the **No Free Lunch theorem** states that if algorithm A outperforms algorithm B on some cost function (or objective function), then loosely speaking there must exist exactly as many other functions where B outperforms A.

In practice optimal algorithm selection is an exploratory process that requires the knowledge of the algorithms as well as the problem domain. Tools that support various sampling methods, enable training and testing of algorithms in customizable workflow, and provide reports on various evaluation measures can greatly enhance the ability of analysts to choose appropriate algorithm that is best for their specific requirements and constraints.

3 Applying Statistics to Predictive Coding

Mark Twain has been attributed with the quotation – "There are three kinds of lies: lies, damned lies, and statistics." Statistics does not lie, but it can be easily applied or interpreted incorrectly if one is not cautious. The intent of this chapter is to provide the proof that statistics can be scientifically applied to predictive coding of natural language documents. The chapter also offers guidance on how to avoid common errors and pitfalls.

Predictive coding technology can be used in a few different ways such as:

- Automatically coding as many documents in the dataset as possible to avoid manual review.
- Crosschecking manually reviewed and classified documents for possible human error. The documents for which human coding and predictive coding disagree can be looked into again for a possible resolution.
- Automatically classifying as many documents in the dataset as possi-

ble into specific category folders and batching them to human reviewers via a specific workflow. Grouping documents based on subject categorization can potentially make the review faster and cost effective. This approach can be very useful, for example, if the case requires different subject matter experts.

This chapter discusses statistical concepts in the context of the first approach, which is the most common use of predictive coding.

Predictive coding can obviously save significant amount of time, effort and money. However, before using predictive coding to bulk-code documents, we want to know how accurate it is. In other words, if we were to have all the documents reviewed and coded manually instead, how closely would the results match to predictive coding? We use statistics to estimate the prediction accuracy and quantify our confidence level in the estimate to a specified margin of error.

To illustrate the statistical concepts, the simple case of binary classification is considered, i.e., documents are classified into categories one at a time. For example, if we need to classify documents into four categories – Responsive, Privileged, Hot Docs, and Other – we first perform predictive coding to classify documents as Responsive and Not-Responsive. Then we classify all the documents as Privileged and Not-Privileged. Finally, we classify all the documents as Hot Docs and Not-Hot Docs. Documents that were not classified into any of the three main categories – Responsive, Privileged and Hot Docs – are then combined and classified into the Other category.

True Classification of Documents

Typically, we use subject matter experts or trained professionals to review and classify documents based on the classification criteria. It is reasonable to expect some amount of human error while reviewing and coding documents. In addition, different reviewers reviewing the same document may disagree on the issue code classification of the document, especially if the criteria are highly subjective. Hence, there is a possibility that there may be no absolute classification of all the documents in a given dataset. The best we can do is to rely on the expert knowledge of human reviewers to classify the documents appropriately, and consider the classification as the true classification of the documents.

Loss Function and Prediction Error Rate

In its simplest form, a function is a computation that takes parameters as input, performs a calculation on that input, and returns the value of the calculation as output. In order to measure the prediction accuracy, we need to define a loss function L for penalizing errors in prediction as follows:

$$L(f(x), h(x)) = \begin{cases} 0 & \text{if } f(x) = h(x) \\ 1 & \text{otherwise} \end{cases}$$

where x is the document, $f(x)$ is true classification of the document (i.e., classification of the document by an expert human reviewer) and $h(x)$ is predicted classification of the document via predictive coding. In simple words, for each document x, $L = 0$ if human reviewer classification and predictive coding classification agree, and $L = 1$ if the two disagree.

A **population** in statistics consists of all elements that are being studied. In our case, the population consists of all documents in the dataset that are being predictively coded. A **parameter** in statistics is defined as a value that represents a certain population characteristic that we are interested in. The parameter we are interested in is prediction error rate, which will be mathematically defined later in this section. Randomness is an important requirement for a sample in statistics. A **simple random sample** is a sample of particular size selected in such a way that each document in the dataset has equal chance of being selected. If the population of documents can be divided into mutually exclusive sub-populations of documents that exhibit certain characteristics, then it is sometimes useful to take a stratified random sample. A **stratified random sample** is taken such that the proportion of documents from each sub-population (referred to as stratum) is maintained. A stratified random sample could be drawn from the population by applying simple random sampling within each stratum.

Let's consider the following example scenario. A dataset D of 100,000 documents needs to be coded Responsive or Non-Responsive. The predictive model was trained using example documents that were provided in addition to the 100,000 documents in the dataset D. A small sample S of 10 documents was randomly drawn from the dataset D. (Note that selecting first 10 documents, for example, would not qualify as a random sample. Selecting 10 document IDs using a random number generator and then fetching the corresponding documents to constitute the sample would qualify as a random sample.) Manual review and coding, and predictive coding were performed on the sample S. The scenario results are shown in the *Table 3.1* below where $f(x)$ denotes the true classification as determined by human reviewer and $h(x)$ denotes the predictive coding classification. The loss function L is computed based on the two values.

Document #	Expert Human Reviewer Classification $f(x)$	Predictive Coding Classification $h(x)$	Loss function $L(f(x), h(x))$
1	Responsive	Responsive	0
2	Non-responsive	Non-responsive	0
3	Responsive	Non-responsive	1
4	Responsive	Responsive	0
5	Responsive	Responsive	0
6	Responsive	Responsive	0
7	Non-responsive	Non-responsive	0
8	Non-responsive	Non-responsive	0
9	Non-responsive	Responsive	1
10	Non-responsive	Responsive	1

Table 3.1: Loss function example

Prediction was incorrect for 3 out of 10 documents (i.e., 30%). We call this the **prediction error rate**. Note that the prediction error rate is also the probability that the loss function L=1 in the sample. Hence, we denote the prediction error rate as p_s and define it via the following mathematical formula:

$$p_s(h) = \frac{1}{n} \sum_{i=1}^{n} L(f(x_i), h(x_i))$$

In simple words, prediction error rate on sample S = Sum of values of L for each document divided by the total number of documents n. Prediction error rate is also referred to as the **overturn rate**.

If we use predictive coding to classify all of 100,000 documents and want to compute the actual prediction error rate, we will need to manually review every single document. It would clearly defeat the purpose of using predictive coding. This is where statistics comes to help. Statistics provides a scientific way of estimating the actual prediction error rate by computing it over a much smaller sample of the dataset. By applying statistics, we can make a mathematically accurate statement as follows:

We are $x\%$ confident that the prediction error rate for the entire population of documents will fall within "sample prediction error rate – margin of error" and "sample prediction error rate + margin of error."

An example of the above statement would look like this: we are 95% confident that the prediction error rate for the entire population of documents will fall within 5% and 10%. This methodology of estimating the actual prediction error rate is reasonably acceptable because, as discussed before, there is a margin of error in classification by human reviewers as well. What the acceptable margin of error is may differ from case to case based on what concerned parties agree upon. Fortunately, statistics also lets us select the margin of error and confidence level that we are comfortable with. Our selection only changes the minimum sample size we need to review manually to estimate the prediction error rate. The minimum sample size does not depend on the size of the population of documents. The following sections describe the derivation of formulas for confidence level, margin of error and sample size.

Binomial Distribution

Before we define binomial distribution, we need to define Bernoulli trial, binomial experiment and probability distribution.

Bernoulli trial

An experiment in which the outcome can be classified into one of two mutually exclusive simple events is called a Bernoulli trial in statistics. Since predictive coding on a document results in either $L = 0$ or $L = 1$, predictive coding is a Bernoulli trial. We are typically interested in one of the two outcomes conventionally referred to as the successful outcome. Since we are interested in finding the prediction error rate, $L = 1$ is the successful outcome. This is not to be interpreted literally as finding more errors equals more success!

Bernoulli experiment

A binomial experiment consists of a fixed number of independent Bernoulli trials that have the same probability of success, and counts the number of successes. Predictive coding qualifies as a binomial experiment because it is performed on a finite number of documents, the outcome $L = 1$ is independent of each document, and the probability that $L = 1$ for a given document is the same.

Probability distribution

A probability distribution is defined as a graph, a table, or a formula that gives the probability of each value of a given random variable. A probability distribution must satisfy the following two conditions:

1. If x is a random variable, then the probability $P(x)$ that x occurs must be between 0 and 1.
2. The sum of probabilities for all values of x must be equal to 1.

The **mean value** μ of a random variable x is defined as the average of all possible values of x weighted by their probabilities $P(x)$, and given by the following mathematical formula:

$$\mu = \sum xP(x)$$

Let's consider a common binomial experiment of tossing a coin 10 times. *Table 3.2* below gives the probabilities of obtaining exactly x Heads on the coin. *Figure 3.1* shows *Table 3.2* plotted on a graph. It is a probability distribution since the probability for each value of x is between 0 and 1, and the sum of all probabilities is 1. The mean value of x, i.e., the average number of Heads in the experiment, is 5. Note that the mean value coincides with the peak of the curve in the graph.

x	$P(x)$
0	0.0009766
1	0.0097656
2	0.0439453
3	0.1171875
4	0.2050781
5	0.2460938
6	0.2050781
7	0.1171875
8	0.0439453
9	0.0097656
10	0.0009766

Table 3.2: *Probabilities for exactly x heads in a coin toss experiment*

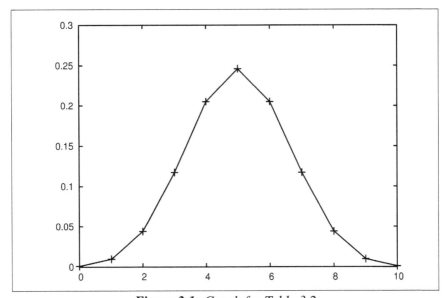

Figure 3.1: *Graph for Table 3.2*

If we perform predictive coding on 10 randomly selected documents, the probability that we get exactly x prediction errors is the probability distribution of predictive coding errors. If the predictive coding algorithm is 50%

inaccurate, then the probability distribution will be the same as *Table 3.2* (or the graph in *Figure 3.1*). If it is 25% inaccurate, then the probability distribution will be as shown in the *Table 3.3* (or the graph in *Figure 3.2*).

x	$P(x)$
0	0.0563135
1	0.1877117
2	0.2815676
3	0.2502823
4	0.1459980
5	0.0583992
6	0.0162220
7	0.0030899
8	0.0003862
9	0.0000286
10	0.0000010

Table 3.3: *Probabilities for exactly x errors for a 25% inaccurate algorithm*

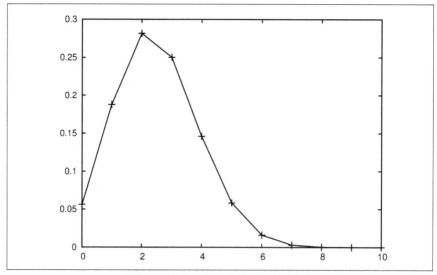

Figure 3.2: *Graph for Table 3.3*

Notice that the curve in the graph shifted to the left when the probability of prediction error is 25%. This makes sense since as the probability of prediction error decreases, so does the mean value of the probability distribution.

The probability distribution of a binomial experiment is referred to as a **binomial distribution**. The following function generates binomial distribution probabilities:

$$P(x) = \frac{n!}{x!(n-x)!} p^x (1-p)^{n-x} \quad for\ x = 0, 1, 2, \ldots, n$$

where x denotes the number of successful outcomes in n trials and p denotes the probability of a successful outcome in a trial. If we know the prediction error rate p for a set of n documents, we can use the above formula to construct the probability distribution of prediction error. However, we will use normal distribution instead for two key reasons:

- Normal distribution is a good approximation for Binomial distribution when the dataset is sufficiently large (more than 30), which is always the case in predictive coding.
- It is much easier to quantify the sampling error for a normal distribution than a binomial distribution in terms of the margin of error for a given confidence level and sample size. Additionally, the formula can be solved to calculate minimum sample size for desired confidence level and margin of error.

Approximation to Normal Distribution

When the number of trials n in a binomial experiment is large (more than 30) and the probability of successful outcome p is not very close to 0 or 1, then the binomial distribution starts to look like the popular bell curve of normal distribution, and normal distribution becomes a good approximation. Detailed information in support of this approximation is outside the scope of this book. However, it can be found in several articles, books and online resources on intermediate to advanced statistics.

Since predictive coding is unlikely to be 100% accurate (prediction error rate p very close to 0) or 100% wrong (prediction error rate p very close to 1), and the number of documents being coded is typically large (from several thousands to over a million) for us to be easily able to draw a random sample of size $n > 30$, the probability distribution of prediction error can be reasonably approximated with a normal distribution function.

Normal distribution is considered as the most important probability distribution in statistics. It is widely used in the natural and social sciences for real-valued random variables whose distributions are not known. Many things closely follow a normal distribution, for example:

- Size of objects produced by machines
- Measurement errors
- Blood pressure
- Exam scores

The following mathematical function generates normal distribution probabilities for a random variable x:

$$P(x) = \frac{1}{\sigma\sqrt{2\pi}} e^{-(x-\mu)^2/2\sigma^2}$$

where $e \cong 2.718$, $\pi \cong 3.14$, μ = mean value of x, and σ = standard deviation of x. **Standard deviation** is a measure of variability in the values of x around the mean value μ. For example, the standard deviation for exam scores with a wide range of values will be high, whereas it will be low if all exam scores are closer to the mean (average) exam score.

Different values of μ and σ yield different normal distributions curves as shown in *Figure 3.3* below.

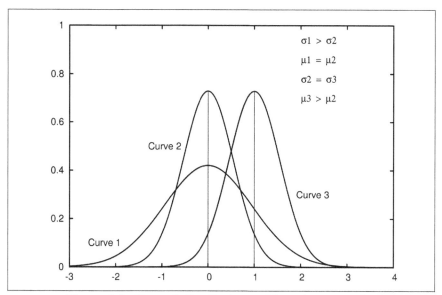

Figure 3.3: Normal distributions with various μ and σ

Although there could be many normal curves, all of them share the following important properties:

1. They are all symmetrical at the center (the mean value).
2. The value of $P(x)$ approaches zero at both ends of the curve but never touches the x-axis.
3. The empirical rule:
   - **One-sigma rule**: 68% of the observations fall within 1 standard deviation of the mean (i.e., between $\mu - \sigma$ and $\mu + \sigma$). In other words, regardless of the shape of the normal distribution, the probability that the value of a normal random variable will be within 1 standard deviation of the mean is approximately equal to 0.68. This is illustrated in *Figure 3.4*.
   - **Two-sigma rule**: 95% of the observations fall within 2 standard deviations of the mean (i.e., between $\mu - 2\sigma$ and $\mu + 2\sigma$). In other words, regardless of the shape of the normal distribution, the probability that the value of a normal random variable will be within 2 standard deviations of the mean is approximately equal to 0.95. This is illustrated in *Figure 3.5*.
   - **Three-sigma rule**: 99.7% of the observations fall within 3 standard deviations of the mean (i.e., between $\mu - 3\sigma$ and $\mu +$

3σ). In other words, regardless of the shape of the normal distribution, the probability that the value of a normal random variable will be within 3 standard deviations of the mean is approximately equal to 0.997. This is illustrated in *Figure 3.6*.

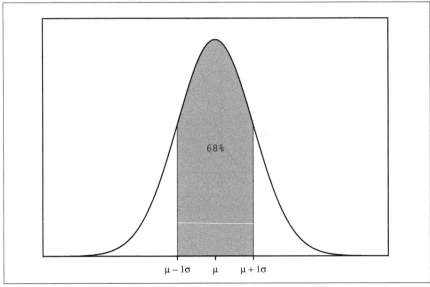

Figure 3.4: *Normal distribution – one-sigma rule*

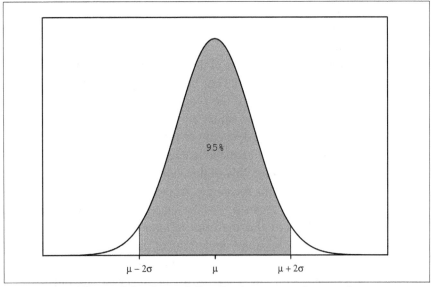

Figure 3.5: *Normal distribution – two-sigma rule*

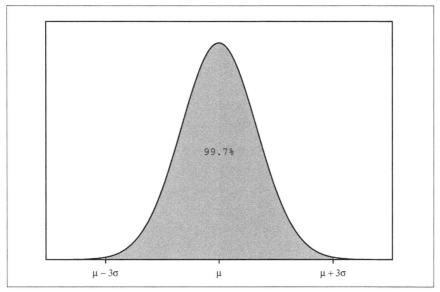

Figure 3.6: Normal distribution – three-sigma rule

Standard Normal Distribution and z-Score

A normal distribution with a mean value of 0 and a standard deviation value of 1 is called as a standard normal distribution. Any normal random variable can be converted to a standard normal random variable by computing the corresponding z-score given by the following formula:

$$z = \frac{x - \mu}{\sigma}$$

The z-score variable has a standard normal distribution. The value of z-score can be interpreted as the number of standard deviation the value of x is more or less than the mean. For example, if $z = 1.5$ for a given value of x, then x is 1.5 times the value of σ.

20 Newsgroups Dataset

Let's analyze the probability distribution of prediction error rate on an example dataset to observe its approximation to normal distribution. The "20 Newsgroups data set" is a collection of approximately 20,000 newsgroup documents partitioned (nearly) evenly across 20 different newsgroups, each corresponding to a different topic, and available in public domain. It has been attributed to Ken Lang, who probably collected it for his Newsweeder: learning to filter netnews paper, though he does not explicitly mention this collection. The 20 newsgroups collection has become a popular data set for experiments in text applications of machine-learning techniques, such as text classification and text clustering. It can be downloaded from the following website: http://qwone.com/~jason/20Newsgroups/. *Table 3.4* below shows a list of the 20 newsgroups, partitioned (more or less) according to subject matter:

comp.graphics comp.os.ms-windows.misc comp.sys.ibm.pc.hardware comp.sys.mac.hardware comp.windows.x	rec.autos rec.motorcycles rec.sport.baseball rec.sport.hockey	sci.crypt sci.electronics sci.med sci.space
misc.forsale	talk.politics.misc talk.politics.guns talk.politics.mideast	talk.religion.misc alt.atheism soc.religion.christian

Table 3.4: *20 Newsgroups dataset partitioned by related topics*

Some of the newsgroups are very closely related to each other (e.g. **comp.sys. ibm.pc.hardware / comp.sys.mac.hardware**), while others are highly unrelated (e.g., **misc.forsale / soc.religion.christian**).

We assume that the documents belonging to a given topic were relevant to that topic ignoring the possibility that a document (message) was mistakenly posted and could be potentially unrelated to the topic. (Note that this is similar to potential human error in coding the documents manually.) In other words, the newsgroups topic labels are assumed to constitute true classification of the documents.

In an experiment, 5 randomly selected documents classified under the topic comp.sys. ibm.pc.hardware were used as examples to train the predictive model. Then predictive coding was performed on the remaining documents in the dataset considered as the population of documents to be coded. The value of loss function was computed for every document in the population based on true classification and predicted classification. The results are summarized in *Table 3.5* below. The prediction error rate for the entire dataset was 5.84%.

Number of Documents	True Classifi- cation $f(x)$	Predicted Classification $h(x)$	Loss function $L(f(x), h(x))$
158	…ibm.pc.hardware	ibm.pc.hardware	0
326	other	…ibm.pc.hardware	1
842	…ibm.pc.hardware	other	1
18671	other	other	0

Table 3.5: *Predictive coding 20 newsgroups dataset for category comp.sys.ibm.pc.hardware*

100 random samples each containing 10 documents were taken from the population, and the prediction error rate was computed for each of the 100 samples. The sampling experiment was repeated for different sample sizes (i.e., the number of documents in each sample) – 50, 100, 500, and 1000 – keeping the number of samples in each set the same (i.e., 100 samples). The graphs for the experiment are shown below:

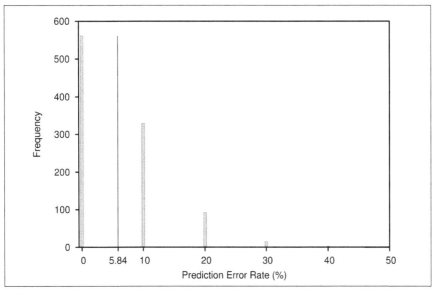

Figure 3.7: *Frequency distribution of prediction error rate in 100 samples, each containing 10 documents*

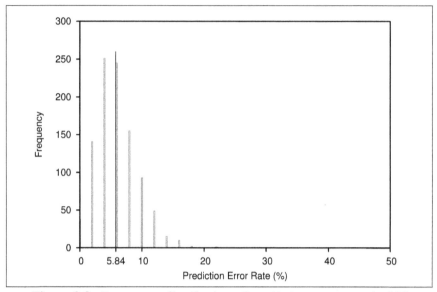

Figure 3.8: *Frequency distribution of prediction error rate in 100 samples, each containing 50 documents*

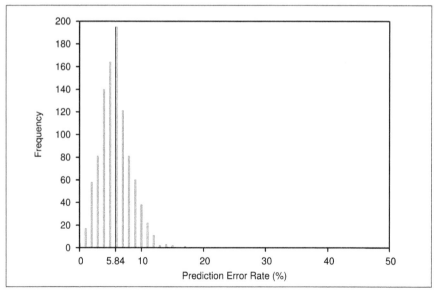

Figure 3.9: *Frequency distribution of prediction error rate in 100 samples, each containing 100 documents*

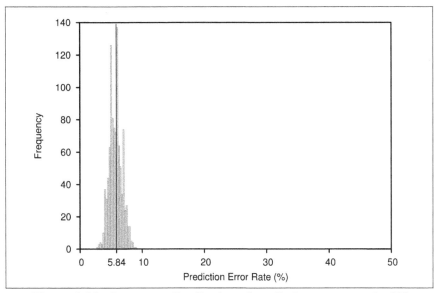

Figure 3.10: *Frequency distribution of prediction error rate in 100 samples, each containing 500 documents*

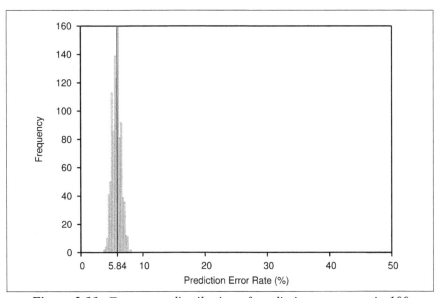

Figure 3.11: *Frequency distribution of prediction error rate in 100 samples, each containing 1000 documents*

Graphs in *Figure 3.7* through *Figure 3.11* illustrate some interesting properties:

- The frequency distribution look like a binomial distribution when the sample size is 10. As the sample size increases, the frequency distribution starts to look like the bell curve of a normal distribution.
- The frequency distribution curves are different for different sample sizes, but their mean value tends to remain the same and close to the prediction error rate for the entire dataset.
- The variance of the curves decreases as the sample size increases, i.e., the variability in the prediction error rate with respect to its mean value decreases as the sample size increases.

The Law of Large Numbers

The Law of Large Numbers states that the average of the results obtained from a large number of trials should be close to the expected value, and will tend to become closer as more trials are performed. The prediction error rate p_D on the entire population of the 20 newsgroups dataset was 5.84 %. *Figure 3.12* below shows the prediction error rate for n documents from a random sample of 1000 documents from the testing on the 20 Newsgroups dataset as n ranges from 1 to 1000.

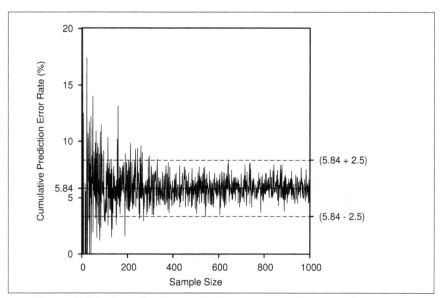

Figure 3.12: *Cumulative prediction error rate in a sample containing 1000 documents*

Notice that the curve converges to the expected value 5.84 (the population prediction error rate p_D) and the variability decreases as the number of trials (the sample size) increases. It also implies that the prediction error rate for a sample p_S is a good estimator for the prediction error rate for the entire population p_D.

Central Limit Theorem for Sample Proportions

Each set (graph) of the random sampling simulation experiment on the 20 newsgroups dataset, for example 1000 samples of size 1000 each, is a frequency distribution of prediction error rate. Such a distribution is referred to as **sampling distribution of a sample proportion** in statistics – sampling distribution because we obtain the distribution from random samples of a specific size, sample proportion because the statistic we are measuring (prediction error rate) is a proportion.

If a random sample of size n is drawn from a population with true proportion p_D (of any attribute of interest such as prediction error rate), and the sample proportion is p_S, the Central Limit Theorem for sample proportions states that for large n ($n > 30$ is considered sufficient), the sampling distribution of the sample proportion:

1. Is approximately normally distributed
2. Is centered at p_D, the true prediction error rate for the document population, which implies $\mu_S = p_D$
3. Has a standard deviation $\sigma_S = \sqrt{p_D(1 - p_D)/n}$

In order to calculate σ_S we need to know p_D. However, the prediction error rate p_D is what we are estimating and its value is unknown. From the Law of Large Numbers, point estimate p_S can be used as a reasonable approximation for p_D. Hence, we can revise the formula for σ_S as follows:

$$\sigma_S \cong \sqrt{p_S(1 - p_S)/n}$$

Confidence Intervals

We stated that p_D is close to p_S as a result of the Law of Large Numbers. We also established in the previous section that the sampling distribution of prediction error rate is approximately normally distributed and figured out the formula to calculate its standard deviation σ_S. Thus, we could apply the two-sigma empirical rule to state that if we repeatedly take random samples S from the population D, 95% of the times, the prediction error rate will fall within 2 standard deviations of the mean, that is, between $\mu_S - 2\sigma_S$ and $\mu_S + 2\sigma_S$. The range of estimate $\mu_S - 2\sigma_S$ and $\mu_S + 2\sigma_S$ is referred to as **confidence interval (CI)** for 95% **confidence level**. Confidence interval can be calculated for any confidence level using a general formula that uses the z-score value. z_α is a z-score such that α area is to the right of z-score value on the bell curve as shown in *Figure 3.13* below.

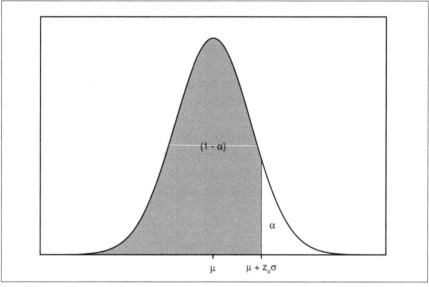

Figure 3.13: *z_α is a z-score such that α area is to the right of z-score value*

z_α value for any given α can be easily obtained from statistical tables or computed via Excel function or statistical library functions available for popular programming languages.

If $\alpha = 5\%$, then $(1 - \alpha) = 95\%$ of the values in the normal distribution. To obtain the 95% confidence interval, we consider the area under the bell curve between $\mu_S - 2\sigma_S$ and $\mu_S + 2\sigma_S$. The sum of remaining area on each side is equal to 5%. Since the normal distribution is symmetrical about its mean value, the area excluded on each side of the 95% confidence interval is half of 5%. Hence, the z-value corresponding to $\mu_S + 2\sigma_S$ is $z_{2.5\%}$. In general, to construct $(1 - \alpha)$ confidence interval we can use $z_{\alpha/2}$ as illustrated in *Figure 3.14* below. (Note that $z_{\alpha/2} \neq z_\alpha/2$.)

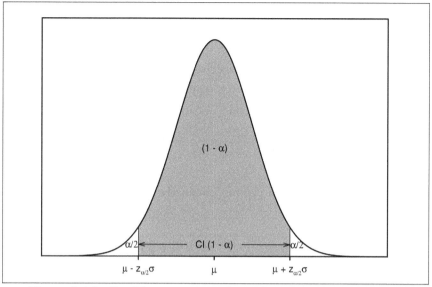

Figure 3.14: *Confidence Interval* $(1 - \alpha)$ *and the corresponding z-value* $z_{\alpha/2}$

Hence, we can state the general formula for constructing a $(1 - \alpha)$ confidence interval for the population prediction error rate as follows:

$$p_S \pm z_{\alpha/2}\sigma_S$$

Substituting the value of $\sigma_S = \sqrt{p_S(1 - p_S)/n}$ we arrived at in the previous section in the above formula gives us:

$$p_S \pm z_{\alpha/2}\sqrt{p_S(1 - p_S)/n}$$

The value $z_{\alpha/2}\sqrt{p_S(1 - p_S)/n}$ is also referred to as the **margin of error** and denoted by letter E. Let's consider one of the samples containing 1000 documents from the testing with 20 newsgroups dataset. The sample prediction error rate was found to be 5.7%. We can use the above formula to determine the 95% confidence interval estimate as follows:

Since n (sample size) = 1000,

$$p_S(sample\ prediction\ error\ rate) = 0.057 = 5.7\%$$
$$(1 - \alpha) = 0.95 = 95\%$$
$$\alpha = 0.05 = 5\%$$
$$z_{\alpha/2} = z_{0.025} = 1.96$$

Hence, the margin of error can be computed as follows:

$$E = \pm z_{\alpha/2}\sqrt{p_S(1 - p_S)/n}$$
$$= \pm 1.96 \times \sqrt{0.057 \times (1 - 0.057)/1000}$$
$$= \pm 0.014$$
$$= \pm 1.4\%$$

and the confidence interval is 4.3% to 7.1%

Thus, we can say that we are 95% confident that the prediction error rate for the entire population of documents would lie between 4.3% and 7.1%.

Sample Size

So far, we always assumed "large enough sample size". But how large is large enough? In the previous section, we derived the following formula for margin of error:

$$E = \pm z_{\alpha/2}\sqrt{p_S(1 - p_S)/n}$$

Notice that E, α and n are related for a given value of p_S. We can solve the above equation for n as follows:

$$n = p_S(1 - p_S)\left(\frac{z_{\alpha/2}}{E}\right)^2$$

The above equation gives the value of minimum sample size for a given value of α, E and p_S. However, we cannot find the value of p_S before taking the sample. $p_S = 0.5$ gives the maximum value for sample size for a given value of α and E because we have $p_S(1 - p_S)$ in the formula. Therefore, we can use the following formula to calculate the upper bound of sample size for the purpose of predictive coding:

$$n = 0.5(0.5)\left(\frac{z_{\alpha/2}}{E}\right)^2 = \left(\frac{z_{\alpha/2}}{2E}\right)^2$$

Notice that the sample size depends on the confidence level and margin of error. However, it **does not** depend on the population size! The sample size for confidence level 95% and margin of error +/-3% is equal to 1067 and this is true for any size of the population. If we want to be 99% confident with a margin of error +/-3%, then the sample size is equal to 1843. The results of the simulated experiments on the 20 newsgroups dataset and the effect of the Law of Large Numbers show that there is some gain in sampling accuracy resulting from increasing sample size. However, once the sample size reaches a certain threshold, there are fewer and fewer accuracy gains derived from further increasing the sample size. This is the reason why Gallup polls and other major polling organizations use sample sizes between 1000 and 1500.

Sampling Error, Sampling Bias and Non-Sampling Error

Sampling error is the deviation in the properties (measured by statistics) of the selected sample from the true properties (measured by parameters) of the population. Sampling error always exists since we are estimating the population parameter on the basis of a much smaller subset of the population in the sample. Sampling error can be eliminated only by observing every element in the population. However, as observed in the sampling simulation experiment on the 20 newsgroups dataset and the illustration of the Law of Large Numbers, the sampling error and its standard deviation reduces as the sample size increases. The sampling error approaches zero as the sample size approaches the population size. As discussed, sampling error can be quantified via constructing confidence intervals for a given sample size.

Sampling bias is a bias in the sample such that some elements of the population are less proportionately represented in the sample. For example, if the sample were taken such that it excluded all PowerPoint files from the population, then it would be a sampling bias. Sampling bias can make the sampling error worse and potentially invalidate statistical inferences based on the sample. Hence, it is important to use a sampling method, such as simple random sampling or stratified random sampling, which is most appropriate for a given population. Below are some example scenarios that can introduce sampling bias in predictive coding process discussed in detail in *Chapter 4*:

- A sampling method or algorithm that does not generate statistically random outcomes
- Native files with partial or incorrect extracted text in the population
- Stratified random sampling on a set of folders that are not mutually exclusive or do not constitute the entire population of documents
- Excluding certain files in the population from sampling based on file type, size, etc. Note that excluding certain files from the population itself does not cause sampling bias.

Non-sampling errors are all other types of errors, including systematic errors and other random errors, which are not caused by the sample itself. Below are some example scenarios that can introduce non-sampling errors in the predictive coding process discussed in detail in *Chapter 4*:

- Including control set elements in example set.
- Changing control set for a given population within a round
- Defining overlapping categories.
- Using same document or text as example for more than one category
- Files with very small amount of text, such as calendar entries, can potentially cause errors.

Summary

1. We started with the premise that we can train a predictive model with some pre-coded example documents and perform predictive coding on the remaining documents in the dataset.

2. In order to measure predictive coding accuracy, we defined a loss function whose value is 0 if expert human classification and predictive coding classification agree, and 1 if the two disagree. We defined prediction error rate as the average value of the loss function over a set of documents.

3. We observed that the probability distribution of the loss function for a sample of documents is a binomial distribution.

4. However, when the number of documents in the sample is large (more than 30), the binomial distribution starts to look more like the normal distribution (the popular bell curve).

5. After analyzing predictive coding results on several samples of various sizes from the 20 newsgroups dataset, we observed that for sample sizes greater than 50, the distribution of prediction error rate for the samples of a given size starts to look like the normal distribution as well.

6. We noted that the Law of Large Numbers in statistics states that as the sample size increases, the sample mean (average) converges to the population (entire dataset) mean. Thus, the prediction error rate for a sample is a good estimator for the prediction error rate for the entire dataset.

7. We found that the observation in point 5 above is a corollary of Central Limit Theorem for sample proportions in statistics. The Central Limit Theorem also provided a formula for the standard deviation of a normal distribution.

8. Having established that the prediction error rate for samples of a large enough sample size is normally distributed with mean and standard deviation given by formulas, we could apply the empirical rule of normal distribution to calculate various confidence intervals.

9. All along we had assumed a large enough sample size. Finally, we derived a formula for sample size required to construct a desired confidence interval.

10. We also discussed sampling errors, sampling bias and non-sampling errors, and how to avoid them.

Thus, we proved that we could perform predictive coding on a random sample of minimum size required for a given confidence level and margin of error, calculate the prediction error rate for the sample, and make a mathematically accurate statement: we have the given confidence level that the prediction error rate for the entire dataset will be equal to the sample prediction error rate +/- the margin of error.

4 Predictive Coding Workflows

There is a lot of confusion in the industry about the right workflow to use for predictive coding. On top of that, every vendor appears to have their own version of the workflow, which is obviously touted as better than the others. The fact that this book introduces yet another workflow might initially dismay some people. However, by the time you finish reading this book, you would feel much better knowing that majority of the workflows currently used in the industry are based on either "Assisted Review Workflow" or "Suggested Review Workflow", or a combination thereof. This chapter provides a lucid explanation of both the workflows highlighting some of the challenges, and introduces a new workflow – "The Greedy Workflow". The greedy workflow takes a locally optimal approach in each iteration of predictive coding resulting in an overall solution that delivers better results. Additionally, the greedy workflow offers significant flexibility and other properties useful in the context of eDiscovery. The greedy workflow was tested on real pre-coded datasets and the detailed results are provided in *Appendix A* and *Appendix B*. The chapter starts with introducing commonly used predictive coding evaluation measures and describes the basic predictive coding process before discussing all the three workflows in detail.

Predictive Coding Evaluation Measures

Predictive coding results can be analyzed using the following **contingency matrix**, also referred to as **confusion matrix**:

	Truly Relevant	**Truly Non-Relevant**	**Row Total**
Predicted Relevant	True Positives (TP)	False Positives (FP)	TP + FP
Predicted Non-Relevant	False Negatives (FN)	True Negatives (TN)	FN + TN
Column Total	TP + FN	FP + TN	n

Table 4.1: Contingency matrix (also referred to as confusion matrix)

The standard evaluation measures used in the industry can be defined in terms of values in the contingency matrix.

The error / accuracy of classifying documents as relevant and non-relevant is given by the following formulas. Note that the prediction error rate defined in *Chapter 3* is essentially the error defined below.

Error = (FP + FN) / (TP + TN + FP + FN)
Accuracy = 100% – Error = (TP + TN) / (TP + TN + FP + FN)

Elusion is defined as the proportion of documents identified as non-relevant that are in fact relevant. Negative predictive value is the opposite of elusion and defined as the proportion of documents identified as non-relevant that are in fact non-relevant.

Elusion = FN / (FN + TN)
Negative Predictive Value = 100% – Elusion = TN / (TN + FN)

Fallout (also referred to as **false positive rate**) is defined as the proportion of non-relevant documents that are incorrectly identified as relevant. True negative rate (also referred to as **specificity**) is the opposite of Fallout and defined as the proportion of non-relevant documents that are correctly identified as non-relevant.

Fallout = FP / (FP+TN)
True Negative Rate = 100% - Fallout = TN / (TN + FP)

Precision (also referred to as **positive predictive value**) is defined as the proportion of documents identified as relevant that are in fact relevant.

Precision = TP / (TP + FP)

Yield (also referred to as **prevalence** or **richness**) is defined as the proportion of documents in a population that are relevant to information need.

Yield = (TP + FN) / (TP + TN + FP + FN)

Recall (also referred to as **true positive rate** or **sensitivity**) is defined as the proportion of relevant documents that are identified as relevant. False negative rate is the opposite of recall and defined as the proportion of relevant documents that are missed (i.e., incorrectly identified as non-relevant)

Recall = TP / (TP+FN)
False Negative Rate = 100% - Recall = FN / (FN+TP)

F-measure (also referred to as **F-score** or **F1-score**) combines both the precision and the recall via a harmonic mean given by the following formula.

F-measure = 2 × (precision × recall) / (precision + recall)

A high F-measure needs both high precision and high recall.

Basic Predictive Coding Process

At a high level, using predictive coding technology to categorize relevant and non-relevant documents, and validating the results with statistics involves the following four elements:

1. **The predictive model.**
2. **A population of documents** that need to be coded. It is assumed that the documents contain textual content that is available in a format suitable for processing by the predictive coding software (typically full text ASCII files in Unicode format).
3. **A control set** which is a random sample of documents taken from the population. The sample size is determined by the desired confidence level and margin of error as discussed in *Chapter 3*.
4. **An example set** that consists of examples for each of the defined categories / issue codes. The examples may comprise of documents from the population, text snippets from the documents, and example text that does not exist as is in any document but provided by subject matter experts based on the relevance criteria of the case. It is assumed that the example set and the control set do not contain any documents in common in order to avoid any bias.

The basic predictive coding process flow is as follows. The example set is used to train the predictive model. The documents in the control set are manually reviewed and coded as relevant or non-relevant. The trained predictive model is run on the control set to test the model. The prediction error rate is computed from predicted coding vs. actual coding on the control set. According to the Central Limit Theorem discussed in *Chapter 3*, predictive coding performance on control set is a good estimator of its performance on the entire population within the confidence interval used to determine the size of the control set. Thus, if the same predictive model is run on the entire population of documents, we are confident to the selected confidence level that we will get the same prediction error rate that we computed for the control set, within the selected margin of error. For example, if we used 95% confidence level and +/- 3% margin of error and found that the prediction error rate on the control set was 10%, then we can state: we are 95% confident that the prediction error rate on the entire population of documents will be between 7% and 13% (i.e., 10% +/- 3%). The Central Limit Theorem generally states that any proportion measured in the sample is a good estimator of the same proportion in the population. Hence, precision, negative predictive value, recall, or any other evaluation measure for the population will also be within the corresponding value computed for the control set +/- margin of error.

The challenge with the basic process flow is that it is highly unlikely in a real life eDiscovery project that we get the necessary and sufficient prediction accuracy on the control set in our first run through the above steps. For example, we may find that the prediction error rate on the control set was 50%, which means that the predictive model was able to get half of the documents coded correctly. This is not good at all. We might as well use a simple program that randomly codes document as relevant or non-relevant. Our simple program will be close to 50% accurate on a large enough population of documents.

Improving Prediction Accuracy

What value of prediction accuracy is necessary and sufficient may vary from case to case and depend on the agreement between the concerned parties. From a technical perspective, prediction accuracy depends on the quality of the example set, the performance of the predictive coding algorithm, and the characteristics of the data itself. Prediction error rate can be lowered for most predictive coding algorithms via the following three approaches:

1. **Improving the example set**: The example set can be improved by adding better examples, removing ineffective examples, and editing examples to remove irrelevant or noisy text. After changes are made to the example set, the predictive model can be retrained and tested for prediction error rate against the same control set. It is useful to keep versions of the example set and the corresponding trained predictive model so that the version delivering lowest prediction error rate can be used.
2. **Adjusting relevance threshold**: Typically, the predictive coding algorithms provide a relevance score for how closely each categorized document is related to one or more example documents of the predicted category. The higher the relevance score of a document, the greater the similarity of the document to the predicted category as a whole. For some algorithms, the relevance score could be based on probability instead of similarity and reflect the probability that a given document belongs to the predicted category. Most predictive coding software products let the user specify minimum relevance threshold score. For example, we can specify that only documents with 80% or more relevance to any of the categories should be predictively coded. A higher relevance threshold returns more documents predicted and fewer documents uncategorized. Higher relevance threshold usually

results in greater precision but this is not always true as observed in test results provided in *Appendix A*. Similarly, prediction error rate may follow a trend or vary unevenly with various relevance threshold levels depending upon the characteristics of the data. Unless the predictive coding software does it automatically, it may be useful to test various values of relevance threshold and select the value that delivers the best result.

3. **Performing iterations**: If additional example documents or text are not available to improve the example set, and adjusting the relevance threshold value does not sufficiently improve the prediction error rate, then the other option is to perform predictive coding iteratively. In traditional workflows, each iteration involves manually reviewing a portion of documents and hence, yields new example documents that could be used to retrain the predictive model. It is important to note that providing more examples to train the predictive model may or may not improve the results from one iteration to the next iteration. However, the number of documents coded relevant continues to increase with each iteration. The iterative cycle ends when the desired accuracy is obtained, in which case the remaining documents are predictively coded, or the estimated total relevant documents have been coded. (Total relevant documents can be estimated from the proportion of relevant documents found in the initial control set sample). The two traditional iterative workflows currently used in the industry are described in the following sections.

Assisted Review Workflow

The assisted review workflow, also referred to as Technology Assisted Review (TAR), is an iterative predictive coding workflow in which the initial example set is improved by utilizing new examples from each iteration. The new examples are obtained via manually reviewing a random sample of documents from the remaining documents that have not been coded. The machine "assists" in randomly selecting the sample of documents to be reviewed in each iteration and predictively coding documents at the end of the iterative cycle if the required minimum accuracy is achieved. The workflow is illustrated in *Figure 4.1* and the steps are described below.

1. Population is defined as the set of documents that are being considered for predictive coding.

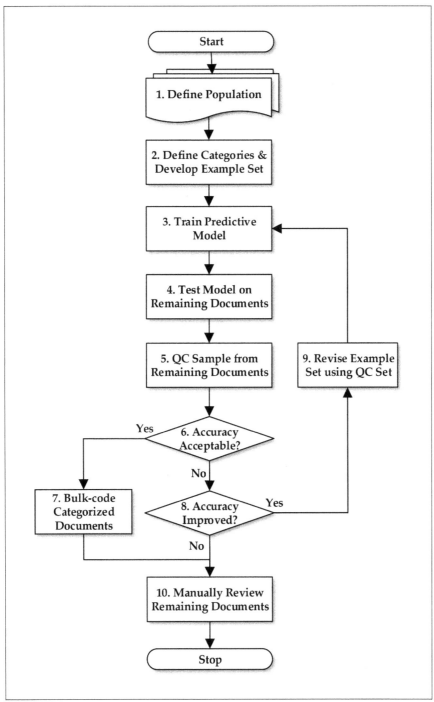

Figure 4.1: *Assisted Review Workflow*

2. One or more categories are defined and example documents are provided for each of the categories. The examples are typically obtained via reviewing a random sample drawn from the population. However, examples could also be obtained via other information retrieval methods or provided by experts knowledgeable of the case. Examples together constitute the example set. This initial example set is also referred to as **seed set**.
3. The predictive model is trained on the example set.
4. The trained model is tested on the remaining documents (i.e., the documents that have not been coded yet.)
5. A quality control (QC) sample is taken from the remaining documents from the previous step and manually reviewed. The QC sample is used for statistical testing and its size is calculated based on the specified confidence level and margin of error.
6. If the prediction accuracy on QC set (calculated based on predicted vs. manually coded category) is acceptable the process moves to step 7, else the process moves to step 8.
7. The categorized documents are bulk-coded with respective predicted categories, and the process moves to step 10.
8. If the prediction accuracy improved compared to the previous iteration the process moves to step 9, else the process moves to step 10.
9. The predictive coding results on QC set are analyzed, and adjustments are made to the example set. Additionally, some of the newly coded documents from the QC set are added as examples to the example set, and the process moves into the next iteration at step 3. This step could be performed manually or by the algorithm automatically.
10. The remaining documents are manually reviewed and coded until the estimated total relevant documents have been coded. At that point the remaining documents are bulk-coded non-relevant, and the process is deemed completed.

Suggested Review Workflow

The other popular workflow, which this book refers to as "Suggested Review Workflow" due to the lack of standard terminology, is an iterative predictive coding workflow in which the initial example set is improved by utilizing new examples from each iteration. The new examples are obtained via manually reviewing a small subset of the remaining documents as "suggested" by the predictive model. The algorithm predictively codes the documents at the end of the iterative cycle if the required minimum accuracy is achieved.

The workflow is illustrated in *Figure 4.2* and the steps are described below:

1. Population is defined as the set of documents that are being considered for predictive coding.

2. One or more categories are defined and example documents are provided for each of the categories. The examples are typically obtained via reviewing a random sample drawn from the population. However, examples could also be obtained via other information retrieval methods or provided by experts knowledgeable of the case. Examples together constitute the example set. This initial example set is also referred to as **seed set**.

3. The predictive model is trained on the example set.

4. The trained model is tested on the remaining documents (i.e., the documents that have not been coded yet.) The predictive model suggests new examples to be manually reviewed and coded in the current iteration. Predictive coding algorithms may use different approaches for making suggestions. Two popular approaches are as follows:

   - **Relevance feedback** - The categorized documents are sorted by their relevance score in descending order. The documents that meet a certain minimum relevance threshold are suggested as new examples. The manual review and coding of suggested examples provides corrective feedback to the system on true relevance of the examples to the predicted category. Relevance feedback can be provided on a binary or graded scale. Binary feedback indicates whether the document is relevant or not. Graded feedback indicates the relevance based on a scale, for example, 1 to 10. Graded scale may also use labels such as "not relevant", "somewhat relevant", "relevant", and "very relevant".

   - **Active learning** – The learning algorithm selects example documents for training based on a strategy, and hence, the argument is that it should take relatively less number of examples to learn a concept compared to normal supervised learning. However, there is a risk that the algorithm is overwhelmed by uninformative examples. Several example selection strategies are possible. **Uncertainty sampling** strategy suggests the examples the algorithm is least certain about as to which category they belong. Expected model change strategy suggests the examples that would change the current predictive model the most. **Expected error reduction** strategy suggests the examples that would reduce the predictive model's generalization error the most.

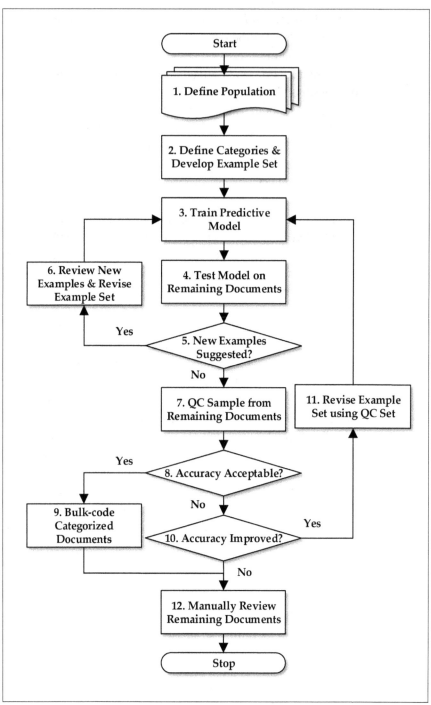

Figure 4.2: Suggested Review Workflow

5. If new examples are suggested by the algorithm in the previous step the process moves to step 6, else the process moves to step 7.
6. The algorithm uses coded examples from step 4 to make adjustments to the example set. The algorithm may also add some of the coded examples to the example set. Then the process moves into the next iteration at step 3.
7. A quality control (QC) sample is taken from the remaining documents in step 4 and manually reviewed. The QC sample is used for statistical testing and its size is calculated based on the specified confidence level and margin of error.
8. If the prediction accuracy on QC set (calculated based on predicted vs. manually coded category) is acceptable the process moves to step 9, else the process moves to step 10.
9. The categorized documents are bulk-coded with respective predicted categories and the process moves to step 12.
10. If the prediction accuracy improved compared to the previous iteration the process moves to step 11, else the process moves to step 12.
11. The predictive coding results on QC set are analyzed, and adjustments are made to the example set. Additionally, some of the newly coded documents from the QC set are added as examples to the example set, and the process moves into the next iteration at step 3. This step could be performed manually or by the algorithm automatically.
12. The remaining documents are manually reviewed and coded until the estimated total relevant documents have been coded. At that point the remaining documents are bulk-coded non-relevant, and the process is deemed completed.

Key Challenges

Workflows based on both the assisted review workflow and the suggested review workflow usually face the following key challenges:

- Both workflows categorize entire population of documents in every iteration. This can take significant amount of computing resources and processing time. It can be avoided in assisted review workflow by drawing the QC sample from the remaining documents first and categorizing only the QC sample to check prediction accuracy. If the prediction accuracy is not acceptable, then the process can move to the next iteration without having to categorize all of the remaining documents. The remaining documents are categorized only at the end of the iterative cycle if it yields acceptable prediction accuracy. However, this solution may not be applicable to the suggested review workflow, because both relevance feedback and active learning approaches may require every document to be categorized in order to find examples to suggest, unless a heuristic approach is employed.

- Both the workflows take the approach of perfecting the predictive model. A perfect solution can be found if all the possible combinations (and edited variations) of example documents are analyzed, but it would be impractical and computationally prohibitive. Hence, the workflows take the practical approach of starting with a seed set and then iteratively improving the predictive model. Since eDiscovery data has complex characteristics, it is often difficult to achieve sufficiently high precision and recall via this approach. Typically, the predictive model reaches a plateau and can no longer be improved after a few iterations. The workflows do not provide a solution if acceptable precision and recall cannot be achieved - in which case, majority of documents could end up being manually reviewed.

- Most derivative workflows currently used in the industry emphasize the use of prediction accuracy (or its complement, prediction error rate or **overturn rate**) as the acceptance criteria. Overturn rate could be potentially misleading. For example, *Table 4.2* below shows predictive coding results on control set of size 1537 from testing conducted on a real dataset (see *Appendix A Round 1.1*).

Relevance Threshold	TP	FP	FN	TN	Precision	Recall	Accuracy
90%	16	50	24	1447	24%	40%	95%

Table 4.2: 95% accuracy with 24% precision and 40% recall

Even though accuracy is 95% (overturn rate 5%), which appears reasonably good at its face value, precision is only 24% and recall is only 40%. If predictive coding is performed on the entire dataset at 90% relevance threshold, it would miss 60% of relevant documents and incorrectly code 76% of non-relevant documents as relevant. It would be clearly unacceptable. Let's assume we were able to remove ineffective examples that predicted 30 false positives and no true positives. Now, we get results shown in *Table 4.3*:

Relevance Threshold	TP	FP	FN	TN	Precision	Recall	Accuracy
90%	16	20	24	1477	44%	40%	97%

Table 4.3: 97% accuracy with precision 44% and recall 40%

Even though accuracy improved to 97% (overturn rate 3%), precision is only 44% and recall stayed at 40%. The reason is that this particular dataset contained very small percentage (2.6%) of relevant documents (based on textual content and not any other rule.) The predictive coding algorithm was able to predict non-relevant documents with much higher accuracy compared to relevant documents, thus achieving a higher overall accuracy rate.

- Training the predictive model with more examples does not necessarily deliver better results as observed in testing results provided in *Appendix A Round 1*.

The Perfect Solution

For a given predictive coding algorithm, the perfect solution would be to find the smallest set of examples that yields a predictive model that perfectly classifies (i.e., with 100% accuracy) the entire dataset into the defined categories. Additionally, the prefect solution must also require the least number of manually reviewed documents as well as the least amount of computing time and resources. A perfect solution may exist and there could potentially be more than one perfect solution for a given dataset. In order to find a perfect solution, we would need to analyze all the possible combinations of examples and their respective prediction accuracy. Finding perfect examples would require manually reviewing all the documents defeating the purpose of predictive coding. Even if all the constraints except perfect classification were dropped, finding a solution would be computationally complex and prohibitive in terms of time, effort and cost.

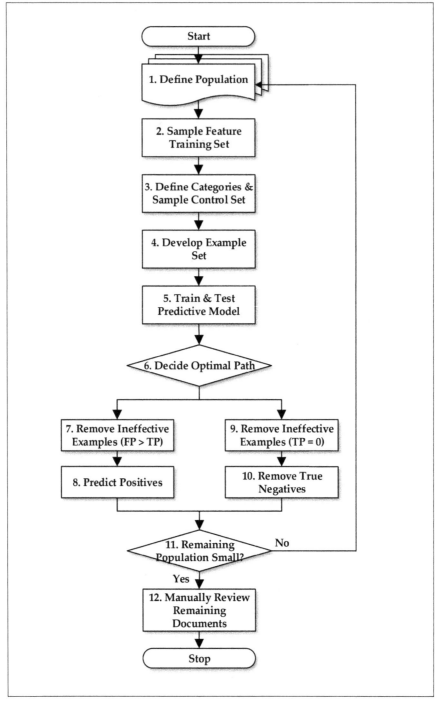

Figure 4.3: The Greedy Workflow

The Greedy Workflow

This book proposes a new workflow for predictive coding that uses the greedy algorithm approach. Greedy algorithms are algorithms that solve a problem by repeatedly executing the same procedure in several rounds and maximizing the return in each round by making the best possible choice based on some criteria. Each round reduces the input size of the problem until the problem is completely solved. Instead of trying to find a globally optimal "perfect" solution, a greedy algorithm finds a locally optimal solution in each round hoping that the overall solution based on the locally optimal solutions approximates a global optimum solution in a reasonable time. The greedy workflow for identifying relevant documents out of a given population of documents is illustrated in *Figure 4.3* and explained below. The workflow was tested on two real pre-coded datasets, one of them containing only Excel files. Detailed results are available in *Appendix A* and *Appendix B*.

1. Define Population
Input:
  • Entire dataset

Output:
  • Defined population of documents

This step defines the population of documents that are being considered for predictive coding in a given round of the greedy workflow. In the initial round, the population of documents is usually the entire dataset or a defined subset of the dataset. It may be useful to segment the entire dataset into subsets containing documents with similar characteristics (not necessarily the characteristics that determine relevance or issue coding) so that each subset can be treated as a separate population for predictive coding. For example, a dataset can be segmented based on custodian, date range, size of textual content, certain file types, or document clusters identified via one of the clustering algorithms. In subsequent rounds, the population of documents is the remaining documents in the initial population that have not been coded yet via either manual review or predictive coding.

It is important to exclude documents that can introduce systematic errors from the initial population. Examples of such documents are as follows:

- Documents that are coded based on metadata (e.g., date range) rather than the relevance of textual content.
- Documents that do not have significant textual content such as images, Excels, charts, etc. If Excels have textual content, it may still be useful to separate them out and treat as a separate population (see *Appendix B*)
- Documents that do not have sufficiently accurate textual content extracted via Optical Character Recognition (OCR)

2. Sample Feature Training Set

Input:

- Population of documents as defined in step 1
- Sample size
- Sampling type – simple random or stratified random

Output:

- Feature training set of documents

This step samples the feature training set of documents to be used to identify important features of documents in the population defined in step 1. Features are used to create the vector space model for a given round of the greedy workflow. As discussed in *Chapter 2*, all documents in the defined population need to be converted into document vectors in a multi-dimensional vector space model, before the predictive coding algorithm can use some documents as examples to categorize other documents into the defined categories. Each dimension of the vector space model represents a feature present in some of the documents in the dataset. The feature could represent a word, a phrase, a combination of words, or a mathematical entity representing a linguistic attribute found in the documents. The feature selection process can be performed on the entire population for the round. Alternatively, some predictive coding software products allow using a sample of documents as feature training set. Using a sufficiently large sample is not such a bad idea because we know that content is repetitive in nature. It may be useful to run clustering algorithm on the population to divide it into mutually exclusive clusters, and then perform a stratified sampling to obtain the feature training set. Stratification can be done by applying simple random sampling on each of the clusters.

3. Define Categories and Sample Control Set

Input:
- Population of documents defined in step 1
- Confidence level
- Margin of error

Output:
- Categories
- Control set of documents
- (Round 1) Estimated target number of relevant documents in the population

This step defines the categories for predictive coding and establishes the control set to be used to test predictive coding performance in the current round. Multiple categories for issue coding can be handled by performing binary classification for each category at a time as described by an example in *Chapter 3*. To simplify the explanation of the workflow, only one category "relevant" is defined and all uncategorized documents are considered "non-relevant".

A random sample of documents is drawn from the population for the control set. As discussed in *Chapter 3*, regardless of the size of the population, the minimum sample size is based on the desired confidence level and margin of error. For example, the minimum sample size for confidence level 95% and margin of error +/-3% is equal to 1067. Typically, it is sufficient to draw a simple random sample without replacement from the population. In a simple random sample, each document in the population has the same probability of being selected in the sample, and the "without replacement" condition requires that a given document be not selected in the sample more than once. Although sampling documents without replacement is no longer independent, it still satisfies exchangeability. Therefore, the generalization of proportions in the sample to proportions in the population holds true. Moreover, if the population size is significantly larger than the sample size, the probability of randomly selecting the same document twice in a sample is very low.

The control set is then reviewed and coded by expert human reviewer as relevant or non-relevant. It is important to make sure that no document is coded both relevant as well as non-relevant. After the review, the proportion

of relevant documents in the control set can be computed which is expected
to be close to the proportion of relevant documents in the population. Thus,
in the first round of the workflow, the target number of relevant documents
is estimated by multiplying the proportion of relevant documents in the
control set with the population size.

4. Develop Example Set

Input:
- Sample documents from the population
- Example text
- Relevant documents or text from previous rounds

Output:
- Example set containing relevant example documents

Example set is the set of example documents, text snippets, or example text
identified as relevant and used to train the predictive model. The testing
on real datasets using this workflow was done using the **lazy approach**:
example set was developed by drawing a simple random sample from the
current round's population, and then selecting documents that were coded
relevant as example documents. However, there is no requirement in terms
of how an example set is developed as long as it is independent from the
control set. (In order to avoid sampling bias, it is very important to make
sure that none of the examples were derived from the control set in the
current round.) Hence, a variety of approaches can be utilized to develop
a good example set. For example, keywords, phrases and example text
can be obtained from attorneys who are knowledgeable of the case. This
text can be used to find more example documents via advanced keyword
search and concept search. Clustering can be applied to the population, and
a stratified random sample can be drawn instead of a simple random sample
to improve the diversity of examples, especially if the dataset is expected to
have sub-populations of documents with particular characteristics.

Typically, drawing a random sample of documents and manually reviewing
them may not yield a significant number of examples. However, a random
sample is an average representation of the population in the current round,
and examples thus chosen usually perform well in training the predictive
model for the round. Relevant documents from previous rounds can also be
used as examples.

5-a. Train Predictive Model

Input:
- Feature training set
- Example set
- Algorithm specific parameters

Output:
- Predictive model

The predictive coding algorithm uses the feature training set to select features for the vector space model. The example documents and text in the example set are converted into vectors of component features in the vector space model. Then the predictive coding algorithm develops a classifier function for the relevant category. The vector space model and the classifier function together constitute the predictive model. The predictive model can be typically saved into a file, which is sometimes referred to as categorization index by some vendors.

5-b. Test Predictive Model on Control Set

Input:
- Predictive model
- Feature training set
- Control set
- Relevance threshold
- Algorithm specific parameters

Output:
- Categorized control set
- Confusion matrix

The predictive coding algorithm uses the feature training set to select features for the vector space model (same as in the previous step). An efficient predictive coding application would perform this step only once and save the feature set in a file that can be reused in this step. The documents in the control set are converted into vectors of component features in the vector space model. Then the predictive coding algorithm runs the classifier function for relevant category developed in the previous step to categorize the documents in the control set. The documents that do not meet the relevance threshold criteria for the relevant category are labeled "uncategorized". The confusion matrix is computed from the categorization results on the control set. This step is repeated with different values of relevance threshold (and other algorithm parameters for advanced use), and the corresponding confusion matrix is computed.

6. Decide Optimal Path
Input:
- Confusion matrix for various relevance thresholds
- Objective function

Output:
- Locally optimal decision
- Optimal relevance threshold value

This is one of the key steps in the greedy workflow. A locally (i.e., for the current round) optimal decision is made based on a user specified objective function to select one of the two paths:

1. **Predict positives**: Categorize some test documents with the relevance threshold value that yielded highest precision. Bulk-code the predicted relevant documents as relevant if acceptable precision was achieved, else manually review and code the predicted relevant documents. Move to step 7.
2. **Remove true negatives**: Categorize all the test documents with the relevance threshold value that yielded total recall (or user specified minimum recall), and bulk-code uncategorized documents as non-relevant. Move to step 9.

The test documents in the current round are the remaining documents in the defined population that have not been coded. In general, we can use relevance threshold that yields 100% precision on the control set to categorize test documents, and bulk-code documents that are predicted relevant as relevant. Similarly, we can use relevance threshold that yields 100% recall on control set to categorize test documents and bulk-code documents labeled "uncategorized" as non-relevant. Since control set is only a statistical random sample, the bulk-coding on the test documents may not be 100% accurate, but we know that it will be accurate within the margin of error.

It is difficult to get 100% precision using predictive coding and without it, the predicted relevant documents will need to be manually reviewed. Still, a high enough precision can yield a significant number of truly relevant documents, which is always desirable when manually reviewing documents. On the other hand, 100% recall is usually possible as the relevance threshold is lowered.

The greedy workflow allows the user to define the objective function used to choose the locally optimal path. Local optimum criteria can be a simple rule or a combination of several rules, for example:

1. Choose remove true negatives path only if recall is 100% and un-categorized documents are at least 5%, else choose predict positives path.
2. Choose remove true negatives path if recall is 97%, else choose predict positives path. Bulk-code predicted relevant as relevant if precision is greater than 90%.

The results from one of the greedy workflow testing rounds in *Appendix A* are shown in *Table 4.4* below:

Relevance Threshold	TP	FP	FN	TN	Precision	Recall	Accuracy
90%	16	50	24	1447	24%	40%	95%
80%	32	379	8	1118	8%	80%	75%
70%	35	869	5	628	4%	88%	43%
60%	40	1142	0	355	3%	100%	26%

Table 4.4: Example greedy workflow round with 100% recall

The size of control set was 1537 corresponding to 95% confidence level and +/-2.5% margin of error. The population size for the round was 216,594. We do not have 100% precision and it seems highly unlikely that there exists a relevance threshold level that would yield 100% precision. On the other hand, we do have 100% recall at 60% relevance threshold.

Let's assume if the objective is to use categorization to bulk-code documents instead of manual review whenever the yield is greater than 10%, which is 21,659 in the above example. 60% relevance threshold gives total (100%)

recall and yields 23% (355 true negatives divided by 1537 documents in control set). Hence, the second path (i.e., remove true negatives) is the locally optimal path and we move to step 9.

There is one important requirement for selecting the optimal relevance threshold. For the first path (i.e., predict positives), the number of predicted relevant documents (i.e., the sum of true positives and false positives) in testing on control set must be at least 30. For the second path (i.e., remove true negatives), the number of uncategorized documents (i.e., the sum of true negatives and false negatives) in testing on control set must be at least 30. The reason for this requirement is the normal distribution approximation.

The results from one of the other rounds from testing in *Appendix A* are shown in *Table 4.5* below:

Relevance Threshold	TP	FP	FN	TN	Precision	Recall	Accuracy
90%	34	72	197	2098	32%	15%	89%
80%	74	220	157	1950	25%	32%	84%
70%	128	505	103	1665	20%	55%	75%
60%	177	942	54	1228	16%	77%	59%
50%	212	1594	19	576	12%	92%	33%
40%	228	2065	3	105	10%	99%	14%
35%	230	2141	1	29	10%	100%	11%
30%	231	2159	0	11	10%	100%	10%

Table 4.5: Example greedy workflow round with poor recall

The size of control set was 2401 corresponding to 95% confidence level and +/- 2% margin of error. The population size for the round was 33,885. Again, we do not have 100% precision and it seems highly unlikely that there exists a relevance threshold level that would yield 100% precision. We do have 100% recall at 30% relevance threshold. However, it yields only 11 uncategorized documents, which is less than the minimum 30 documents. It also does not meet the objective function criteria of a minimum 10% yield. Hence, the first path (i.e., predict positives) is the locally optimal path and we move to step 7.

7. Remove Ineffective Examples (FP > TP)

Input:
- Predictive model
- Control set
- Relevance threshold with highest precision
- Algorithm specific parameters

Output:
- Confusion matrix
- Optimal relevance threshold value

This step is optional and only applicable if the predictive coding application offers ability to identify the example document or documents responsible for predicting test documents in the control set as relevant. Precision value can be improved by removing ineffective examples that predicted more false positives than true positives (i.e., FP > TP). The predictive model needs to be updated after the ineffective examples are removed. This may require rebuilding the predictive model depending upon the algorithm and the application. Then the predictive model is tested again on the control set for the relevance threshold value that yields the best precision. The number of predicted relevant documents (i.e., sum of true positives and false positives) in testing on the control set must be at least 30. The corresponding relevance threshold is the optimal value and used in the next step.

Note that depending upon the algorithm and the dataset, this step may or may not result in improvement in precision value. Removing the ineffective examples may cause some of the test documents that were predicted because of them to be now predicted by other (effective) examples. For instance, if nearest neighbor approach is used, one of the effective examples (which happened to be the next nearest neighbor within the threshold distance) could now predict a false positive test document that was initially predicted by an ineffective example. Thus, this step is discarded if the precision value does not improve, and the results from the previous step are used in the next step.

8. Predict Positives

Input:

- Predictive model
- Test set
- Review batch size
- Optimal relevance threshold from the previous step

Output:
- Test documents predicted relevant sent for manual review
- Uncategorized test documents constitute the remaining population

If the optimal relevance threshold from the previous step yielded 100% precision (or other acceptable precision value), then we can bulk-code the remaining documents predicted relevant as truly relevant without manually reviewing them. However, it is difficult to get close to 100% precision, hence we are likely going to have to review the documents that are predicted relevant. At this point, the decision can be made on the **review batch size**, i.e., the number of documents we want to review in this round. The **test documents sample size** required to yield the review batch is equal to review batch size divided by percentage of predicted relevant documents in the control set. For example, if the review batch size is 3000 documents and 100 documents were predicted relevant in control set of 1537 (i.e. 6.51%), then the test documents sample size that would yield 3000 predicted relevant documents = 3000/6.51% = 46,083. If the total number of test documents is less than 46,083 then we categorize all of remaining documents, else we draw a simple random sample of 46,083 documents from the remaining documents and categorize only the sample.

The predictive coding algorithm uses the vector space model created from the feature training set to convert the selected test documents into vectors of component features. Then the predictive coding algorithm runs the classifier for relevant category at the optimal relevance threshold from the previous step to categorize the selected test documents. The test documents that are predicted relevant are sent for manual review. The test documents that are left uncategorized constitute the new remaining population. The process moves to step 11.

9. Remove Ineffective Examples (TP = 0)
Input:
- Predictive model
- Control set
- Highest relevance threshold with 100% (or other acceptable) recall

- Algorithm specific parameters

Output:
- Confusion matrix
- Optimal relevance threshold value

This step is optional and only applicable if the predictive coding application offers ability to identify the example document or documents responsible for predicting test documents in the control set as relevant. The number of true negatives can be improved by removing ineffective examples that predicted only false positives (i.e., TP=0). The predictive model needs to be updated after the ineffective examples are removed. This may require rebuilding the predictive model depending upon the algorithm and the application. Then the predictive model is tested again on the control set for the highest relevance threshold value that yields 100% (or other acceptable) recall. The number of uncategorized documents (i.e., the sum of true negatives and false negatives) in testing on control set must be at least 30. The corresponding relevance threshold is the optimal value and used in the next step.

Note that depending upon the algorithm and the dataset, this step may or may not result in improvement in the number of true negatives. The reason is same as in the case of step 7 although this step will not affect recall value since none of the effective examples that predicted the true positives are removed. This step is discarded if the number of true negatives does not improve, and the results from the previous step are used in the next step.

10. Remove True Negatives
Input:
- Predictive model
- Test set
- Optimal relevance threshold from the previous step

Output:
- Uncategorized test documents coded non-relevant
- Test documents predicted relevant constitute the remaining population

The predictive coding algorithm uses the vector space model created from the feature training set to convert all the test documents into vectors of component features. Then the predictive coding algorithm runs the classifier for relevant category at the optimal relevance threshold from the previous step to categorize the test documents. The test documents that remain uncategorized are bulk-coded as non-relevant. The test documents that are predicted relevant constitute the remaining population. The process moves to step 11.

11. Check Size of Remaining Population
Input:
- Remaining population

Output:
- Yes/No

If the remaining population is greater than the sum of the size of example set and control set samples to be drawn in the next round, then it is set as the defined population for the next round, and the process is iterated by going to step 1. Otherwise, the process moves to the next and final step.

12. Manually Review Remaining Documents
Input:
- Remaining population

Output:
- All documents coded

The remaining population is manually reviewed and the workflow stops since all documents have been coded.

Key Properties of Greedy Workflow

The greedy workflow offers several useful properties and a lot of flexibility to the user in terms of the choices that can be made in each round. The key properties are described below:

1. The greedy workflow approach always terminates with all the documents coded.
2. The completion of workflow is agnostic to manual review errors. If some documents were misclassified as relevant or non-relevant due to errors in manual review, it would naturally affect the precision of the algorithm, and 100% recall may also be difficult to obtain at a reasonable true negative yield. The workflow will still continue

to progress although it might take more rounds to complete. The workflow also does not propagate manual review errors from one round to the next round, because each round has a new control set.

3. Confidence interval, and hence, the sample size can be changed in any round. Low yield datasets may require a bigger sample size in initial rounds in order to have at least 30 relevant documents in the random sample. The yield may increase in later rounds as true negatives are removed, and hence the sample size can be reduced to the minimum required size (based on minimum acceptable confidence interval).

4. Acceptable recall value for removing true negatives can be changed in any round. For example, 99% recall may be acceptable instead of 100% recall because the documents in control set that could not be recalled were found weakly relevant.

5. Any precision value for predicting positives can be selected in a given round. For instance, 90% relevance threshold may deliver 50% precision but predict only 4% of control set documents as relevant. On the other hand, 80% relevance threshold may deliver 35% precision but predict 15% of control set documents as relevant. If the remaining documents are only 20,000 and the optimal review batch size based on the available number of reviewers is 3000, then using 90% relevance threshold will result in about 800 documents for manual review. On the other hand, 80% relevance threshold will result in about 3,000 documents. Hence, considering total time and cost, it would be optimal to go with 80% relevance threshold even though the precision is lower.

6. "Remove ineffective examples (FP > TP)" can be skipped if yield of predicted relevant is less than the review batch size. If "Remove ineffective examples (FP > TP)" step is performed at 80% relevance threshold in the previous example, it would likely reduce the % predicted documents and hence, result in less than 3000 documents for manual review.

7. Any objective function can be defined based on the goals and constraints of the project, and can be changed in any round if needed.

8. Algorithm specific parameters can be changed and fine-tuned in any round if necessary.

9. The workflow supports rolling collection (rolling ingestion), a process in which new potentially relevant documents are identified and added to the dataset even while it is in review stage. New set of documents can be added at the beginning of any round since a round always starts with a new defined population.

10. The workflow supports rolling production, a process in which relevant documents are delivered incrementally to the requesting party. Every round results in some documents coded as relevant.

Additionally, predictive coding application could automate several parts of the workflow, e.g., parameterizing the above decision points, automating the calculation of optimal relevance threshold based on those parameters, and automatically removing / suppressing ineffective examples when useful.

Why does Greedy Workflow Work Well?

The greedy workflow works well because of the following two key reasons:

1. **Iterative problem reduction**: The greedy workflow breaks down the categorization problem into rounds, each round working on a different defined population. The defined population in any given round has unique data characteristics. The most important features extracted from the population and used for the vector space model are based on those data characteristics. The best possible classifier function produced by the predictive coding algorithm in that round is used to either predict positives or remove true negatives based on user's objective function or choice. The remaining documents become the defined population for the next round. This new population has somewhat different data characteristics than the previous round's population. This results in a new set of important features and a new vector space model. The predictive coding algorithm produces a new classifier function for the new vector space model. Each round reduces the number of remaining documents to be coded. Finally, the workflow terminates with the full solution of all documents coded accurately within the margin of error.

2. **Local optimization**: It is easier for the predictive coding algorithm to find a locally optimal classifier function with a new vector space model in each round of reduced dataset, rather than a globally optimal classifier solution on the vector space model of the entire dataset. Local optimization also offers flexibility, because the optimal choice can be based on several parameters such as acceptable precision for bulk-coding predicted positives, acceptable recall for bulk-coding predicted negatives, bulk-coding yield, categorization processing time & resources, manual review optimization, production requirements, etc.

Dos and Don'ts

Dos

- Initial culling based on criteria such as domain, file type, date range, deNIST, etc. can significantly reduce the size of the dataset as well as improve the yield. Categorization takes significant computing time and resources, and the algorithm used may not be linearly scalable. Hence, reducing the dataset size, when possible, is always helpful.
- If yield is very low (less than 2%) and culling is not an option, the dataset can be segmented using a variety of techniques such as clustering, keyword searches, file types, etc., utilizing the relevance criteria. Predictive coding can be performed on dataset segments that have greater yield. This approach enables rolling production. After sufficient number of relevant documents have been produced, the remaining very low yield dataset segments may not need to be reviewed depending upon the case protocol. Segmenting dataset is also helpful and sometimes unavoidable if the dataset is too big to be processed by the predictive coding algorithm all at once.
- If the control set or the example set random sample does not fetch at least 30 relevant documents, the sample size should be increased.
- Global de-duplication could be performed without the loss of custodian information, and only one copy of each document included in the dataset for predictive coding.
- Mutually exclusive categories and mutually exclusive examples for those categories would improve predictive coding results.
- Coding based on document family relationship should be performed after the completion of predictive coding workflow.

Don'ts

- Do not change example set while the corresponding predictive model is being tested against the control set. This would help avoid any discrepancy.
- Do not change feature training set and control set within a round.
- Do not use control set for examples. Control set and example set must remain statistically independent to avoid bias.
- Do not include files with partial or incorrect extracted text or very small amount of text in the population for predictive coding.

A Test Results on Real Dataset

The greedy workflow presented in this book was tested on a real pre-coded dataset. The dataset had a total of 288,137 documents tagged with one of the following tags – Responsive, Responsive A, Responsive B and Non-Responsive.

Following information regarding the dataset was not available:
- Document parent-child (family) relationship
- Duplicate identification
- Responsiveness criteria

Because of the missing information, there is a possibility that some documents were pre-coded as responsive or non-responsive based on criteria other than the responsiveness of their textual content, for example, family relationship, date range, etc.

Some documents were excluded from this test as described in *Table A.1*:

Documents	Excluded	Included
Excel files (based on file extension, e.g., .xls, .xlsx, .xlt)	45,699	
Files and image files with less than 100 bytes of extracted full text	25,781	
Tagged both Responsive and Non-Responsive	63	
Tagged Responsive only		5161
Tagged Non-Responsive only		211,433
Total	**71,543**	**216,594**

Table A.1: Real dataset 1 files included / excluded for greedy workflow testing

The final set of 216,594 documents was considered as the initial population of documents for predictive coding in this experiment. All documents tagged Responsive, Responsive A, or Responsive B were considered True Positives. All documents tagged Non-Responsive were considered True Negatives. Binary categorization was used. Only one category "Responsive" was defined for all types of responsive documents. All uncategorized documents were considered predicted non-responsive. Each round started with new examples obtained from a simple random sample drawn from that round's defined population of documents. All the true positive documents in the sample were used as examples as is without any editing. Multiple iterations were performed in rounds 1 and 2 to study and illustrate the effect of adding more examples to the example set and retraining the predictive model based on the same vector space model for that round.

While the "problem reduction" approach was followed for every round, several other parameters involved in the greedy workflow – confidence level, margin of error, feature training set size, greedy objective function and the decision on "predict positives" vs. "remove true negatives" path, and review batch size – were changed in different rounds in order to study and illustrate their effect. Note that the greedy workflow will complete regardless of what choice is made in step 6 of every round, and whether the choice is optimal or not. The results of testing are summarized in *Table A.2* and details on each round are provided in subsequent sections.

#	Round / Step	Population	Manually Reviewed	Bulk-Coded	FN	TP
1.1	Sample, Train & Test	216,594	3074			80
1.2	Predict Positives	213,520	933			166
1.3	Predict Positives	212,587	882			237
1.4	Remove True Negatives	211,705		53,202	189	
2.1	Sample, Train & Test	158,503	3074			77
2.2	Predict Positives	155,429	984			128
2.3	Remove True Negatives	154,445		65,267	136	
3.1	Sample, Train & Test	89,178	3074			145
3.2	Remove True Negatives	86,104		32,640	221	
4.1	Sample, Train & Test	53,464	4802			370
4.2	Remove True Negatives	48,662		5757	55	
5.1	Sample, Train & Test	42,905	4802			367
5.2	Remove True Negatives	38,103		4218	68	
6.1	Sample, Train & Test	33,885	4802			415
6.2	Predict Positives	29,083	563			328
7.1	Sample, Train & Test	28,520	3074			218
7.2	Predict Positives	25,446	112			82
8.1	Sample, Train & Test	25,334	3074			215
8.2	Remove True Negatives	22,260		2701	23	
9.1	Sample, Train & Test	19,559	3074			245
9.2	Predict Positives	16,485	2838			570
10.1	Sample, Train & Test	13,647	3074			186
10.2	Predict Positives	10,573	2430			301
11.1	Sample, Train & Test	8143	3074			128
11.2	Manual Review	5069	5069			213
	Totals		**52,809**	**163,785**	**692**	**4471**
	%		**24.38%**	**75.62%**	**0.32%**	**2.06%**

Table A.2: *Test Results Summary for Dataset 1*

Round 1.1 Sample, Train & Test

- Confidence level = 95%
- Margin of error = +/- 2.5%
- Defined population size = 216,594
- Feature training set size = 21,659
- Sample size for control set = 1537
- Responsive documents found in control set = 40
- Sample size for example set = 1537
- Example set size (responsive documents in the above sample) = 40

Relevance Threshold	TP	FP	FN	TN	Precision	Recall	Accuracy	Uncategorized
90%	16	50	24	1447	24%	40%	95%	96%
80%	32	379	8	1118	8%	80%	75%	73%
70%	35	869	5	628	4%	88%	43%	41%
60%	40	1142	0	355	3%	100%	26%	23%

Table A.3: Round 1.1 results of predictive coding on control set for various relevance thresholds

Even though 100% recall was achieved at 60% threshold and removing true negatives appeared to be the locally optimal path that would enable bulk-tagging 23% of remaining documents as non-responsive, the other path of predicting positives was taken to analyze the effect of adding more of "similar" examples to the current round's vector space model.

Round 1.2 Predict Positives

No "ineffective examples" were removed. Review batch size was assumed to be 1000 documents, and hence the test documents sample size was calculated to be 23,288 based on 4.3% predicted responsive. Same predictive model was run on the test documents sample at relevance threshold of 90%. 933 test documents were predicted responsive. Only 166 out of the 933 were truly responsive (true positives).

- Remaining documents = 213,520
- Review batch size = 1000

- Test documents sample size = 23,288
- Relevance threshold = 90%
- Predicted responsive = 933
- True positives = 166

Instead of moving into the next round, the 166 true positives were added to the example set of the current round containing 40 examples. The predictive model was retrained and tested on the same control set. The idea was to test if adding true positives to the example set improves the predictive model for current round's vector space model. The results were as follows:

- Example set size = 166 + 40 = 206
- Control set = (same as before)

Results of predictive coding on control set for various relevance thresholds:

Relevance Threshold	TP	FP	FN	TN	Precision	Recall	Accuracy	Uncategorized
90%	26	100	14	1397	21%	65%	93%	92%
80%	33	496	7	1001	6%	83%	67%	66%
70%	36	926	4	571	4%	90%	39%	37%

Table A.4: *Round 1.2 results of predictive coding on control set for various relevance thresholds*

The precision got slightly worse at 21% with more examples. At this point "ineffective examples (FP > TP)" were removed at relevance threshold of 90%. The predictive model was retrained and tested on the same control set. The results were as follows:

- Removed ineffective examples = 45
- Example set size = 206 - 45 = 161
- Control set = (same as before)

Results of predictive coding on control set for various relevance thresholds:

Relevance Threshold	TP	FP	FN	TN	Precision	Recall	Accuracy	Uncategorized
90%	24	36	16	1461	40%	60%	97%	96%
80%	33	383	7	1114	8%	83%	75%	73%
70%	36	844	4	653	4%	90%	45%	43%
60%	40	1119	0	378	3%	100%	27%	25%

Table A.5: Round 1.2 results of predictive coding on control set for various relevance thresholds after removing ineffective examples (FP > TP)

The precision increased from 21% to 40%. 100% recall was achieved at 60% threshold and removing true negatives once again appeared to be the locally optimal path that would enable bulk-tagging 25% of remaining documents as non-responsive. However, the other path of predicting positives was given one more try. The objective was again to test if more examples could potentially yield significantly better results on the same vector space model.

Round 1.3 Predict Positives

Review batch size was again assumed to be 1000 documents, and hence the test documents sample size was calculated to be 25,617 based on 3.9% predicted responsive. Same predictive model was run on the new test documents sample at relevance threshold of 90%. 886 test documents were predicted responsive. Only 237 out of the 886 were truly responsive (true positives).

- Remaining documents = 212,587
- Review batch size = 1000
- Test documents sample size = 25,617
- Relevance threshold = 90%
- Predicted responsive = 886
- True positives = 237

Instead of moving into the next round, the 237 true positives were added to the example set from round 1.2 containing 161 examples. The predictive model was retrained and tested on the same control set. The idea was to test if a second iteration of adding true positives to the example set improves the predictive model for current round's vector space model. The results were as follows:

- Example set size = 161 + 237 = 398
- Control set = (same as before)

Results of predictive coding on control set for 90% relevance threshold:

Relevance Threshold	TP	FP	FN	TN	Precision	Recall	Accuracy	Uncategorized
90%	27	71	13	1426	28%	68%	95%	94%

Table A.6: Round 1.3 results of predictive coding on control set for various relevance thresholds

With yet more examples, the precision came below 40% but improved slightly at 28% compared to 21% before ineffective examples were removed. "Ineffective examples (FP > TP)" were removed from the total example set again at relevance threshold of 90%. The predictive model was retrained and tested on the same control set. The results were as follows:

- Removed ineffective examples = 49
- Example set size = 398 – 49 = 349
- Control Set = (same as before)

Results of predictive coding on Control Set for various relevance thresholds:

Relevance Threshold	TP	FP	FN	TN	Precision	Recall	Accuracy	Uncategorized
90%	27	49	13	1448	36%	68%	96%	95%
80%	33	461	7	1036	7%	83%	70%	68%
70%	36	886	4	611	4%	90%	42%	40%
60%	40	1153	0	344	3%	100%	25%	22%

Table A.7: Round 1.3 results of predictive coding on control set for various relevance thresholds after removing ineffective examples (FP > TP)

The precision increased from 28% to 36% but still came lower than the highest 40% observed in the previous iteration. The precision did not improve consistently with more examples, and it seemed highly unlikely to achieve acceptable precision even with several more iterations. Hence, it was decided to continue with the optimal greedy path of removing true negatives.

Round 1.4 Remove True Negatives

The predictive model from round 1.2 at relevance threshold 60% delivered 100% recall with highest uncategorized documents (25%). Hence, it was used to remove true negatives. The results were as follows:

- Remaining documents = 211,705
- Relevance threshold = 60%
- Example set size = 161
- Uncategorized documents bulk-coded non-responsive = 53,202
- False negatives in bulk-coded documents = 189
- Population for next round = documents predicted responsive = 158,503

Note that 189 false negatives were found in 53,202 documents that were bulk-coded as non-responsive. This is within the margin of error +/-2.5%.

Round 2.1 Sample, Train & Test

- Confidence level = 95%
- Margin of error = +/- 2.5%
- Defined population size = 158,503
- Feature training set size = 15,850
- Sample size for control set = 1537
- Responsive documents found in control set = 42
- Sample size for example set = 1537
- Example set size (responsive documents in the above sample) = 35

Results of predictive coding on control set for various relevance thresholds:

Relevance Threshold	TP	FP	FN	TN	Precision	Recall	Accuracy	Uncategorized
90%	1	10	41	1485	9%	2%	97%	99%
80%	2	29	40	1466	6%	5%	96%	98%
70%	9	78	33	1417	10%	21%	93%	94%
60%	23	186	19	1309	11%	55%	87%	86%
50%	30	334	12	1161	8%	71%	77%	76%
40%	40	655	2	840	6%	95%	57%	55%

Table A.8: Round 2.1 results of predictive coding on control set for various relevance thresholds

100% recall could not be achieved even when relevance threshold was dropped to 40%. Although it was likely that we could have achieved 100% recall at 30% relevance threshold and TN count was still looking pretty good, we were not yet convinced of the goodness of the greedy workflow. Hence, we decided to go with the other path of predicting positives.

Round 2.2 Predict Positives

No "ineffective examples" were removed. Review batch size was assumed to be 1000 documents, and hence the test documents sample size was calculated to be 7354 based on 13.6% predicted responsive. Same predictive model was run on the test documents sample at relevance threshold of 60%. 1004 test documents were predicted responsive. Only 128 out of the 1004 were truly responsive (true positives).

- Remaining documents = 155,429
- Review batch size = 1000
- Test documents sample size = 7354
- Relevance threshold = 60%
- Predicted responsive = 1004
- True positives = 128

The 128 true positives were added to the example set from round 2.1 containing 35 examples. The predictive model was retrained and tested on the same control set. The results were as follows:

- Example set size = 128+35 = 163
- Control set = (same as before)

Results of predictive coding on control set for various relevance thresholds:

Relevance Threshold	TP	FP	FN	TN	Precision	Recall	Accuracy	Uncategorized
90%	2	15	40	1480	12%	5%	96%	99%
80%	12	48	30	1447	20%	29%	95%	96%
70%	20	131	22	1364	13%	48%	90%	90%
60%	29	268	13	1227	10%	69%	82%	81%

Table A.9: Round 2.2 results of predictive coding on control set for various relevance thresholds

With yet more examples, the precision improved to 20%. "Ineffective examples (FP > TP)" were removed at relevance threshold of 80%. The predictive model was retrained and tested on the same control set. The results were as follows:

- Removed ineffective examples = 22
- Example set size = 163 − 22 = 141
- Control set = (same as before)

Results of predictive coding on control set for various relevance thresholds:

Relevance Threshold	TP	FP	FN	TN	Precision	Recall	Accuracy	Uncategorized
80%	12	30	30	1465	29%	29%	96%	97%
70%	19	120	23	1375	14%	45%	91%	91%
60%	28	261	14	1234	10%	67%	82%	81%
50%	34	472	8	1023	7%	81%	69%	67%
40%	42	825	0	670	5%	100%	46%	44%
35%	42	1046	0	449	4%	100%	32%	29%

Table A.10: *Round 2.2 results of predictive coding on control set for various relevance thresholds after removing ineffective examples (FP > TP)*

The precision increased from 20% to 29% but did not improve sufficiently, and it seemed highly unlikely to achieve acceptable precision even with several more iterations. However, we got 100% recall at 40% relevance threshold. Hence, it was decided to continue with the optimal greedy path of removing true negatives.

Round 2.3 Remove True Negatives

The predictive model from round 2.2 at relevance threshold 40% delivered 100% recall with highest uncategorized documents (44%). Hence, it was used to remove true negatives. The results were as follows:

- Remaining documents = 154,445
- Relevance threshold = 40%
- Example set size = 141
- Uncategorized documents bulk-coded non-responsive = 65,267
- False negatives in bulk-coded documents = 136
- Population for next round = documents predicted responsive = 89,178

Note that 136 false negatives were found in 65,267 documents that were bulk-coded as non-responsive. This is within the margin of error +/-2.5%.

Round 3.1 Sample, Train & Test
- Confidence level = 95%

- Margin of error = +/- 2.5%
- Defined population size = 89,178
- Feature training set size = 8918
- Sample size for control set = 1537
- Responsive documents found in control set = 66
- Sample size for example set = 1537
- Example set size (responsive documents in the above sample) = 79

Results of predictive coding on control set for various relevance thresholds:

Relevance Threshold	TP	FP	FN	TN	Preci- sion	Re- call	Accu- racy	Uncatego- rized
90%	2	13	64	1458	13%	3%	95%	99%
80%	14	57	52	1414	20%	21%	93%	95%
70%	31	124	35	1347	20%	47%	90%	90%
60%	47	288	19	1183	14%	71%	80%	78%
50%	62	631	4	840	9%	94%	59%	55%
40%	66	1056	0	415	6%	100%	31%	27%

Table A.11: *Round 3.1 results of predictive coding on control set for various relevance thresholds*

100% recall was achieved at 40% relevance threshold and 27% uncatego-rized, which could be bulk-coded as non-responsive. Hence, we decided to go with the remove true negatives path in this round. In order to boost the true negative count at 100% recall, "ineffective examples (TP = 0)" were removed at relevance threshold of 40%. The predictive model was retrained and tested on the same control set. The results were as follows:

- Removed ineffective examples = 37
- Example set size = 79 – 37 = 42
- Control set = (same as before)

Results of predictive coding on control set for various relevance thresholds:

Relevance Threshold	TP	FP	FN	TN	Precision	Recall	Accuracy	Uncategorized
40%	66	881	0	590	7%	100%	43%	40%

Table A.12: Round 3.1 results of predictive coding on control set for various relevance thresholds after removing ineffective examples (TP = 0)

Uncategorized documents increased from 27% to 40%.

Round 3.2 Remove True Negatives

The predictive model from round 3.1 at relevance threshold 40% was used to remove true negatives. The results were as follows:

- Remaining documents = 86,104
- Relevance threshold = 40%
- Example set size = 42
- Uncategorized documents bulk-coded non-responsive = 32,640
- False negatives in bulk-coded documents = 221
- Population for next round = documents predicted responsive = 53,464

Note that 221 false negatives were found in 32,640 documents that were bulk-coded as non-responsive. This is within the margin of error +/-2.5%.

Round 4.1 Sample, Train & Test

- Confidence level = 95%
- Margin of error = +/- 2%
- Defined population size = 53,464
- Feature training set size = 5347
- Sample size for control set = 2401
- Responsive documents found in control set = 184
- Sample size for example set = 2401
- Example set size (responsive documents in the above sample) = 186

Results of predictive coding on control set for various relevance thresholds:

Relevance Threshold	TP	FP	FN	TN	Precision	Recall	Accuracy	Uncategorized
90%	36	101	148	2116	26%	20%	90%	94%
50%	180	1562	4	655	10%	98%	35%	27%
40%	184	2080	0	137	8%	100%	13%	6%

Table A.13: *Round 4.1 results of predictive coding on control set for various relevance thresholds*

100% recall was achieved at 40% relevance threshold and 6% uncategorized, which could be bulk-coded as non-responsive. Hence, we decided to go with the remove true negatives path in this round. In order to boost the true negative count at 100% recall, "ineffective examples (TP = 0)" were removed at relevance threshold of 40%. The predictive model was retrained and tested on the same control set. The results were as follows:

- Removed ineffective examples = 84
- Example set size = 186 − 84 = 102
- Control set = (same as before)

Results of predictive coding on control set for various relevance thresholds:

Relevance Threshold	TP	FP	FN	TN	Precision	Recall	Accuracy	Uncategorized
40%	184	1936	0	281	9%	100%	19%	12%

Table A.14: *Round 4.1 results of predictive coding on control set for various relevance thresholds after removing ineffective examples (TP = 0)*

Uncategorized documents increased from 6% to 12%.

Round 4.2 Remove True Negatives

The predictive model from round 4.1 at relevance threshold 40% was used to remove true negatives. The results were as follows:

- Remaining documents = 48,662
- Relevance threshold = 40%
- Example set size = 102
- Uncategorized documents bulk-coded non-responsive = 5757
- False negatives in bulk-coded documents = 55
- Population for next round = documents predicted responsive = 42,905

Note that 55 false negatives were found in 5757 documents that were bulk-coded as non-responsive. This is within the margin of error +/-2%.

Round 5.1 Sample, Train & Test

- Confidence level = 95%
- Margin of error = +/- 2%
- Defined population size = 42,905
- Feature training set size = 8000
- Sample size for control set = 2401
- Responsive documents found in control set = 195
- Sample size for example set = 2401
- Example set size (responsive documents in the above sample) = 195

Results of predictive coding on control set for various relevance thresholds:

Relevance Threshold	TP	FP	FN	TN	Precision	Recall	Accuracy	Uncategorized
90%	20	52	153	2176	28%	12%	91%	97%
80%	58	178	115	2050	25%	34%	88%	90%
50%	163	1549	10	679	10%	94%	35%	29%
40%	173	2089	0	139	8%	100%	13%	6%

Table A.15: Round 5.1 results of predictive coding on control set for various relevance thresholds

100% recall was achieved at 40% relevance threshold and 6% uncategorized, which could be bulk-coded as non-responsive. Hence, we decided to go with the remove true negatives path in this round. In order to boost the true negative count at 100% recall, "ineffective examples (TP = 0)" were removed at relevance threshold of 40%. The predictive model was retrained and tested on the same control set. The results were as follows:

- Removed ineffective examples = 80
- Example set size = 195 – 80 = 115
- Control set = (same as before)

Results of predictive coding on control set for various relevance thresholds:

Relevance Threshold	TP	FP	FN	TN	Precision	Re-call	Accu-racy	Uncatego-rized
40%	173	1982	0	246	8%	100%	17%	10%

Table A.16: *Round 5.1 results of predictive coding on control set for various relevance thresholds after removing ineffective examples (TP = 0)*

Uncategorized documents increased from 6% to 10%.

Round 5.2 Remove True Negatives

The predictive model from round 5.1 at relevance threshold 40% was used to remove true negatives. The results were as follows:

- Remaining documents = 38,103
- Relevance threshold = 40%
- Example set size = 115
- Uncategorized documents bulk-coded non-responsive = 4218
- False negatives in bulk-coded documents = 68
- Population for next round = documents predicted responsive = 33,885

Note that 68 false negatives were found in 4,218 documents that were bulk-coded as non-responsive. This is within the margin of error +/-2%.

Round 6.1 Sample, Train & Test

- Confidence level = 95%
- Margin of error = +/- 2%
- Defined population size = 33,885

- Feature training set size = 8000
- Sample size for control set = 2401
- Responsive documents found in control set = 231
- Sample size for example set = 2401
- Example set size (responsive documents in the above sample) = 184

Results of predictive coding on control set for various relevance thresholds:

Relevance Threshold	TP	FP	FN	TN	Precision	Recall	Accuracy	Uncategorized
90%	34	72	197	2098	32%	15%	89%	96%
80%	74	220	157	1950	25%	32%	84%	88%
70%	128	505	103	1665	20%	55%	75%	74%
60%	177	942	54	1228	16%	77%	59%	53%
50%	212	1594	19	576	12%	92%	33%	25%
40%	228	2065	3	105	10%	99%	14%	4%
35%	230	2141	1	29	10%	100%	11%	1%
30%	231	2159	0	11	10%	100%	10%	0%

Table A.17: *Round 6.1 results of predictive coding on control set for various relevance thresholds*

100% recall (zero FN) was achieved at 30% relevance threshold but the FN count was very low. Hence, predicting positives path was taken in this round. "Ineffective examples (FP > TP)" were removed at relevance threshold of 90%. The predictive model was retrained and tested on the same control set. The results were as follows:

- Removed ineffective examples = 18
- Example set size = 184 − 18 = 166
- Control set = (same as before)

Results of predictive coding on control set for various relevance thresholds:

Relevance Threshold	TP	FP	FN	TN	Preci-sion	Re-call	Accu-racy	Uncatego-rized
90%	32	12	199	2158	73%	14%	91%	98%
80%	71	121	160	2049	37%	31%	88%	92%

Table A.18: Round 6.1 results of predictive coding on control set for various relevance thresholds after removing ineffective examples (FP > TP)

The precision increased from 32% to 73%.

Round 6.2 Predict Positives

Since the % predicted documents was small (1.8%), all of remaining documents were categorized via the predictive model from round 6.1 at relevance threshold of 90%. 563 test documents were predicted responsive. Only 328 out of the 563 were truly responsive (true positives).

- Remaining documents = 29,083
- Review Batch size = 1000
- Test documents sample size = 29,083 (everything)
- Relevance threshold = 90%
- Predicted responsive = 563
- True positives = 328

Round 7.1 Sample, Train & Test

- Confidence level = 95%
- Margin of error = +/- 2%
- Defined population size = 28,520
- Feature training set size = 8000
- Sample size for control Set = 1537
- Responsive documents found in Control Set = 118
- Sample size for example Set = 1537
- Example set size (responsive documents in the above sample) = 100

Results of predictive coding on control set for various relevance thresholds:

Relevance Threshold	TP	FP	FN	TN	Precision	Recall	Accuracy	Uncategorized
90%	5	10	113	1409	33%	4%	92%	99%
80%	18	101	100	1318	15%	15%	87%	92%
70%	42	262	76	1157	14%	36%	78%	80%
60%	78	500	40	919	13%	66%	65%	62%
50%	104	905	14	514	10%	88%	40%	34%
40%	113	1218	5	201	8%	96%	20%	13%
30%	115	1346	3	73	8%	97%	12%	5%

Table A.19: *Round 7.1 results of predictive coding on control set for various relevance thresholds*

100% recall (zero FN) was not achieved at 30% and FN count already dropped very low. Hence, predict positives path was taken in this round. "Ineffective examples (FP > TP)" were removed at relevance threshold of 90%. The predictive model was retrained and tested on the same control set. The results were as follows:

- Removed ineffective examples = 7
- Example set size = 100 – 7 = 93
- Control set = (same as before)

Results of predictive coding on control set for various relevance thresholds:

Relevance Threshold	TP	FP	FN	TN	Precision	Recall	Accuracy	Uncategorized
90%	4	0	114	1419	100%	3%	93%	100%
80%	13	70	105	1349	16%	11%	89%	95%
70%	39	232	79	1187	14%	33%	80%	82%
60%	73	470	45	949	13%	62%	66%	65%

Table A.20: *Round 7.1 results of predictive coding on control set for various relevance thresholds after removing ineffective examples (FP > TP)*

Highest precision increased from 33% to 100%. Hence, predict positives path was chosen at 90% threshold that yielded 100% precision. (At this point in our experimentation, the condition that the minimum number of predicted responsive documents must be 30 for normal distribution approximation had not been established. The requirement was confirmed after some more parallel testing with other test data also showed that the generalization of sample proportions to population proportions did not work so well when the number of documents in the sample corresponding to the proportion was very low. The threshold level of minimum 30 documents was chosen to be on the conservative side and was applied in later rounds of testing.)

Round 7.2 Predict Positives

Since the % predicted documents was small (0.2%), all of remaining documents were categorized via the predictive model from round 7.1 at relevance threshold of 90%. 112 test documents were predicted responsive. Only 82 out of the 112 were truly responsive (true positives).

- Remaining documents = 25,446
- Review batch size = 1000
- Test documents sample size = 25,446 (everything)
- Relevance threshold = 90%
- Predicted responsive = 112
- True positives = 82

Round 8.1 Sample, Train & Test

- Confidence level = 95%
- Margin of error = +/- 2.5%
- Defined population size = 25,334
- Feature training set size = 8000
- Sample size for control set = 1537
- Responsive documents found in control set = 109
- Sample size for example set = 1537
- Example set size (responsive documents in the above sample) = 106

Results of predictive coding on control set for various relevance thresholds:

Relevance Threshold	TP	FP	FN	TN	Precision	Recall	Accuracy	Uncategorized
90%	7	17	102	1411	29%	6%	92%	98%
80%	21	98	88	1330	18%	19%	88%	92%
70%	34	216	75	1212	14%	31%	81%	84%
40%	100	1244	9	184	7%	92%	18%	13%
35%	108	1343	1	85	7%	99%	13%	6%
30%	109	1392	0	36	7%	100%	9%	2%

Table A.21: Round 8.1 results of predictive coding on control set for various relevance thresholds

100% recall was achieved at 30% relevance threshold and 2% uncategorized – a low number, but we decided to go with the remove true negatives path in this round. In order to boost the true negative count at 100% recall, "ineffective examples (TP = 0)" were removed at relevance threshold of 30%. The predictive model was retrained and tested on the same control set. The results were as follows:

- Removed ineffective examples = 46
- Example set size = 106 – 46 = 60
- Control set = (same as before)

Results of predictive coding on control set for various relevance thresholds:

Relevance Threshold	TP	FP	FN	TN	Precision	Recall	Accuracy	Uncategorized
30%	109	1250	0	178	8%	100%	19%	12%

Table A.22: Round 8.1 results of predictive coding on control set for various relevance thresholds after removing ineffective examples (TP = 0)

Uncategorized documents increased from 2% to 12%.

Round 8.2 Remove True Negatives

The predictive model from round 8.1 at relevance threshold 30% was used to remove true negatives. The results were as follows:

- Remaining documents = 22,260
- Relevance threshold = 30%
- Example set size = 60
- Uncategorized documents bulk-coded non-responsive = 2701
- False negatives in bulk-coded documents = 23
- Population for next round = documents predicted responsive = 19,559

Note that 23 false negatives were found in 2701 documents that were bulk-coded as non-responsive. This is within the margin of error +/-2.5%.

Round 9.1 Sample, Train & Test

- Confidence level = 95%
- Margin of error = +/- 2.5%
- Defined population size = 19,559
- Feature training set size = 8000
- Sample size for control set = 1537
- Responsive documents found in control set = 109
- Sample size for example set = 1537
- Example set size (responsive documents in the above sample) = 112

Results of predictive coding on control set for various relevance thresholds:

Relevance Threshold	TP	FP	FN	TN	Precision	Recall	Accuracy	Uncategorized
90%	12	12	121	1392	50%	9%	91%	98%
80%	27	72	106	1332	27%	20%	88%	94%
70%	49	225	84	1179	18%	37%	80%	82%
40%	132	1270	1	134	9%	99%	17%	9%
35%	132	1346	1	58	9%	99%	12%	4%

Table A.23: Round 9.1 results of predictive coding on control set for various relevance thresholds

100% recall (zero FN) was not achieved at 35% and FN count already dropped very low. Hence, predict positives path was taken in this round. "Ineffective examples (FP > TP)" were removed at relevance threshold of 70% because % predicted count for both 90% and 80% relevance threshold was very low and would have resulted in fewer documents than the desired review batch size. The predictive model was retrained and tested on the same control set. The results were as follows:

- Removed ineffective examples = 34
- Example set size = 112 – 34 = 78
- Control set = (same as before)

Results of predictive coding on control set for various relevance thresholds:

Relevance Threshold	TP	FP	FN	TN	Precision	Recall	Accuracy	Uncategorized
90%	11	0	122	1404	100%	8%	92%	99%
80%	22	1	111	1403	96%	17%	93%	99%
70%	38	22	95	1382	63%	29%	92%	96%

Table A.24: Round 9.1 results of predictive coding on control set for various relevance thresholds after removing ineffective examples (FP > TP)

Precision for 70% relevance threshold increased from 18% to 63%.

Round 9.2 Predict Positives

Since the % predicted documents was small (3.9%), all of remaining documents were categorized via the predictive model from round 9.1 at relevance threshold of 70%. 2838 test documents were predicted responsive. Only 570 out of the 2838 were truly responsive (true positives).

- Remaining documents = 16,485
- Review batch size = 1000
- Test documents sample size = 16,485 (everything)
- Relevance threshold = 70%
- Predicted responsive = 2838

- True positives = 570

Round 10.1 Sample, Train & Test

- Confidence level = 95%
- Margin of error = +/- 2.5%
- Defined population size = 13,647
- Feature training set size = 8000
- Sample size for control set = 1537
- Responsive documents found in control set = 101
- Sample size for example Set = 1537
- Example set size (responsive documents in the above sample) = 85

Results of predictive coding on control set for various relevance thresholds:

Relevance Threshold	TP	FP	FN	TN	Precision	Recall	Accuracy	Uncategorized
90%	12	11	89	1425	52%	12%	93%	99%
80%	21	29	80	1407	42%	21%	93%	97%
70%	26	105	75	1331	20%	26%	88%	91%
60%	41	310	60	1126	12%	41%	76%	77%
50%	83	789	18	647	10%	82%	47%	43%
40%	99	1257	2	179	7%	98%	18%	12%
35%	99	1362	2	74	7%	98%	11%	5%

Table A.25: *Round 10.1 results of predictive coding on control set for various relevance thresholds*

100% recall (zero FN) was not achieved at 35% and FN count already dropped very low. Hence, predict positives path was taken in this round. "Remove ineffective examples (FP > TP)" step was skipped because % predicted number was already low and fewer remaining documents were left to be coded.

Round 10.2 Predict Positives

All of remaining documents were categorized via the predictive model from round 10.1 at relevance threshold of 60%. 2430 test documents were predicted responsive. Only 301 out of the 2430 were truly responsive (true positives).

- Remaining documents = 10,573
- Review batch size = 1000
- Test documents sample size = 10,573 (everything)
- Relevance threshold = 60%
- Predicted responsive = 2430
- True positives = 301

Round 11.1 Sample, Train & Test

- Confidence level = 95%
- Margin of error = +/- 2.5%
- Defined population size = 8143
- Feature training set size = 8143
- Sample size for control set = 1537
- Responsive documents found in control set = 67
- Sample size for example set = 1537
- Example set size (responsive documents in the above sample) = 61

Results of predictive coding on control set for various relevance thresholds:

Relevance Threshold	TP	FP	FN	TN	Precision	Recall	Accuracy	Uncategorized
90%	3	18	64	1452	14%	4%	95%	99%
80%	7	36	60	1434	16%	10%	94%	97%
70%	9	73	58	1397	11%	13%	91%	95%
60%	14	218	53	1252	6%	21%	82%	85%
50%	40	568	27	902	7%	60%	61%	60%
40%	62	1107	5	363	5%	93%	28%	24%
30%	65	1388	2	82	4%	97%	10%	5%

Table A.26: *Round 11.1 results of predictive coding on control set for various relevance thresholds*

Since a high precision with high % predicted, or 100% recall with high % uncategorized could not be achieved, and the remaining documents were sufficiently low 5069 to be manually reviewed, the greedy workflow rounds were concluded. After manually coding the last 5069 documents, all documents had been coded.

Analysis of Results

With every round of reduced population of documents, the greedy workflow developed a new vector space model and was always able to find a new classifier function. The greatest gains were had when 100% recall was achieved with a high FN count. This enabled not only knocking out large number of non-responsive documents but also improved the yield (richness) of the remaining dataset to be used as population for the following round. The documents that were reviewed manually when the predict positives path was taken contained more responsive documents (to the extent the best classifier function for the corresponding round could produce). In most cases, it is desirable to utilize human reviewer resources on a richer batch of documents. The other advantage is that the batch size could be used to throttle the process flow and optimize not only the utilization of computing resources (by not having to categorize entire dataset in every round) but also human resources (by using the optimum work order quantity for the review team size and the average review rate). The greedy workflow delivered impressive performance by predictively coding 76% of the documents with 100% precision (assuming no human review error) and 87% recall. The number of rounds could have been fewer if the responsiveness criteria were known since the examples documents in each round could have been edited to remove non-responsive or noisy content. The false negatives (missed responsive documents) could be explained via the following possibilities:

- None of the false negatives were highly relevant documents.
- Many false negatives may be similar to each other, which would further reduce the proportion of information lost.
- Some of the documents were coded responsive based on family relationship or other metadata rather than responsiveness of the textual content.

B Test Results on Excel Dataset

The second test was performed to see how well the greedy workflow does on only Excel data. A new pre-coded dataset from a real case containing a total of 364,453 potentially responsive documents was selected for the experiment. The dataset contained 93,982 Excel files. The data was very complex not only because of large number of Excels but also foreign language content. The 93,982 Excel files were considered as the initial population of documents for predictive coding. Following information regarding the dataset was not available:

- Document parent-child (family) relationship
- Responsiveness criteria

Because of the missing information, there is a possibility that some documents were pre-coded as responsive or non-responsive based on criteria other than the responsiveness of their textual content, for example, family relationship, date range, etc.

The results of testing are summarized in *Table B.1* below:

#	Round / Step	Population	Manually Reviewed	Bulk-Coded	FN	TP
1.1	Sample Ex & Cntl Set	93,982	3074			242
1.2	Predict Positives	90,908	1157			386
2.1	Sample Ex & Cntl Set	89,751	3074			206
2.2	Remove True Negatives	86,677		7671	196	
3.1	Sample Ex & Cntl Set	79,006	3074			252
3.2	Remove True Negatives	75,932		5229	158	
4.1	Sample Ex & Cntl Set	70,703	3074			257
4.2	Remove True Negatives	67,629		6785	172	
5.1	Sample Ex & Cntl Set	60,844	3074			284
5.2	Remove True Negatives	57,770		4708	248	
6.1	Sample Ex & Cntl Set	53,062	3074			283
6.2	Remove True Negatives	49,988		6857	307	
7.1	Sample Ex & Cntl Set	43,131	3074			295
7.2	Remove True Negatives	40,057		7731	247	
8.1	Sample Ex & Cntl Set	32,326	3074			329
8.2	Remove True Negatives	29,252		4042	163	
9.1	Sample Ex & Cntl Set	25,210	3074			401
9.2	Remove True Negatives	22,136		1304	62	
10.1	Sample Ex & Cntl Set	20,832	4802			579
10.2	Remove True Negatives	16,030		2541	86	
11.1	Sample Ex & Cntl Set	13,489	4802			667
11.2	Remove True Negatives	8687		945	67	
	Manual Review	7742	7742			1150
	Totals		**46,169**	**47,813**	**1706**	**5331**
	%		**49.13%**	**50.87%**	**1.82%**	**6%**

Table B.1: *Test Results Summary for Dataset 2 containing only Excels*

All documents tagged Responsive were considered True Positives. All documents tagged Non-Responsive were considered True Negatives. Binary categorization was used. Only one category "Responsive" was defined for responsive documents. All uncategorized documents were considered predicted non-responsive. Each round used new examples obtained from a simple random sample drawn from that round's defined population of documents. All the true positive documents in the sample were used as examples as is without any editing. Responsive documents identified in the previous rounds were not used as examples. The greedy workflow was strictly followed with the following objective function: "Remove true negatives" if 97% recall is achieved, and it yields true negatives greater than 10% of the population for that round; else "predict positives" for manual review.

Index

www.ingramcontent.com/pod-product-compliance
Lightning Source LLC
Chambersburg PA
CBHW071212050326
40689CB00011B/2307